10 x 50

500 Tips, Tools, & Techniques to Maximize Your Youth Ministry

ISBN 0-9663339-0-X

Evans, Paul
Millergren, AL

10 x 50
500 Tips, Tools, and Techniques
To Maximize Your Youth Ministry

Morris Publishing
3212 East Highway 30
Kearney, NE 68847
1-800-650-7888

Table of Contents

Table of Contents

10 x 50

Within these pages are 500 tips, tools, & techniques to help you maximize your ministry. Don't be surprised if a lot of these sound like common sense because they are. We didn't write a book that contained ideas no one could use, this book is practical. Our goal is to follow the example of Jesus who said "Now that you know these things, you will be blessed if you do them" (John 13:17).

Each idea is followed by a brief description, summary, or way to use it. This information is practical and may or may not fit your specific position at this time in your ministry. That's why you have 500 ideas to choose from. Something will hit you right where you are! (probably most of it).

Use these tips to help you get the most out of 10 x 50.

Tip #1 *Read with a highlighter.* Make a point glow so you won't overlook it. Come back to it again and keep it fresh in your mind.

Tip #2 *Use the margins.* If you'll notice, the margins are extra wide. If a tip, tool, or technique comes to mind while reading, write it in. If an idea comes to mind on how to apply the tip, scribble it in the margin.

Tip #3 *Apply.* As you read you might be thinking, "I ought to try that." Yep! But thinking about it isn't the same as doing it. Put the ideas to use. They can't maximize your ministry on the page, but they can when practiced.

Maximize Your Ministry!

Paul Evans & Al Millergren, Ph.D.

ONE

10 GOALS FOR YOUTH MINISTRY

1 **Do whatever it takes to get teens to heaven.** Paul wrote that he became all things to all people so that some might be saved (II Corinthians 9:19-23). How well does this relate to your ministry? What could you be doing that might reach more teens in your schools and community?

Ministry has its own set of pressures. We have to worry about what the leaders, parents, and members will think about a program or event. By doing whatever it takes to get teens to heaven, you will endure your share of criticism about your approaches, but keep the goal in focus. Keep everyone involved aware that you are not using a certain technique just to be different, but to bring teens to Jesus.

2 **Help teens develop a personal relationship with God.** While second-hand faith is better than no faith, there's no doubt that first-hand faith wins the prize. Help teens develop a faith that says, "I believe in God, not because my parents say so, or because my youth minister or preacher says so, but because I have experienced and know God in my life."

3 **Involve teens in daily Bible study and prayer.** Instead of simply asking your group to read the Bible and pray daily, provide the opportunity and tools to make it possible. Develop a daily Bible reading schedule for your teens. Supply information on Bibles designed for youth so they can get a grip on the Word in a way relevant to them.

Form prayer groups of three that meet at school, or that call each other daily for prayer requests. Challenge your group to pray before getting out of bed and before going to sleep. Have teens set their watch alarms for a certain time each day to signal prayer time. Create as many tools as needed to get them into the Bible and prayer on a daily basis.

4. **Build a Christ-like attitude and spirit into the youth group.** "Your attitude should be the same as that of Christ Jesus," Philippians 2:5. This means more than just asking, "What would Jesus do?" It calls for a clear-cut lifestyle of surrender. What is the attitude of Jesus?

- Attitude of a Servant (v. 7)
- Attitude of Humility (v. 8)
- Attitude of Obedience (v. 8)

If every teen becomes a servant, how many things will get done? If every teen becomes humble, how much arguing will take place? If every teen becomes obedient to God, how much better could the youth conventions be? Of course, developing a Christ-like attitude in your group begins by displaying a Christ-like attitude in your life.

5. **Develop quality leadership among the group.** Jesus called His followers with, "Follow me." By the end of His ministry He had trained them to lead. Paul even said, "Imitate me as I imitate Christ" (I Corinthians 11:1). Give your teens the responsibility and let them lead. Dust them off when they fall down and encourage them to keep going.

Here are a few ways you can let teens lead: Devotionals, teaching class, heading up a service project, forming prayer groups, etc.

6. **Parental support and participation.** Believe it or not, There are some in your congregation who see youth ministry as a divider of parents and their children. Prevent this by creating a high level of parental involvement.

Have your parents teach for a quarter, host devotionals in their homes, chaperone trips, etc. Check out Group Publishing's *130 Ways to Involve Parents in Your Ministry* for more great ideas.

7 **Develop evangelistic teens.** Redirect the vision of your group by training them to see each classmate, each neighbor, each family member, each clerk, each waiter, just fill in the blank, each ____________ as an opportunity to share the Lord.

Jesus left the message in our mouths and lives. Help your group become evangelistic by creating an atmosphere that makes guests want to return. Go out to the school campus and meet kids on their turf. Be available, open and loving.

8 **Establish positive relationships with other youth groups in the area.** If we are not careful ministry can become a competition where the leader with the most teens wins. Because of that, we may be afraid to do things with other groups for fear that our teens might spot something "cooler" than what we provide. Don't forget #4 and build a Christ-like attitude by doing things with other groups like retreats or prayer nights. One of the easiest ways to establish positive relationships is by participating together in community events such as the *March for Jesus,* or collecting food and toys for needy families during the holidays.

9 **Include teens as part of the congregation.** Have you ever felt the perception that there is the church, and then there is the youth group? Integrate the group into the congregation by getting the teens involved in praying, scripture reading, or whatever format your church follows. Most churches let teens participate on youth days. But encourage your leadership to include teens on a regular basis, not just special days.

10 **Equip teens to go into all the world and teach the Gospel.** While every teen has the responsibility to evangelize around them, a few feel the call to literally go into all the world. Prepare them for that future by encouraging and praying for him or her. Help sponsor teens on a yearly mission trip to gain experience. Provide contacts through special mission organizations to get teens involved. Who knows how many will come to know the Lord as a result of your ministry.

TWO

10 Priorities for a Successful Ministry

1 **Depend completely on God.** God alone never fails. At some time everyone has felt the hurt of a broken trust. We all know the sting of death or the sharp criticism of a friend. And then there's God - always keeping His promises, providing strength in weakness, dispensing comfort in painful times, pouring forgiveness on the sinful heart.

Memorize Proverbs 16:7, "Commit to the Lord whatever you do, and your plans will succeed." Make God's plans your plans. Make His will the only will you desire. Want what God wants.

2 **Always give God the glory for all successes.** "Great job!" "We couldn't make it around here without you." "I just can't thank you enough for what you have done for Jonathan." "That's the best retreat I've ever been on!"

With an abundance of praise comes the temptation of pride. Instead of hogging it, our light should shine in such a way that people see what good things we do and give God the credit (Matthew 5:16).

3 **Never give up on a teen.** You never know when something might click within the heart of a young person. That kid who gets strung out on marijuana every Friday night might become your next leader through God's grace. That girl who possesses the unspiritual gift of gossip might be molded into the greatest proclaimer of God's truth in her school when God transforms her.

When all within you wants to give in and give up on a certain misfit or misguided teen, remember Jonah. It took three uncomfortable days to change his ways, but God did it. Think about Saul who went from prosecuting to being persecuted for the kingdom. Consider the prodigal son who wasted all his father gave him, and yet dad waited on the edge of the property for his boy's return. And who could forget us? Certainly there was a time when we gave our Father reason to give up...but he didn't.

4 **Build relationships with those on the fringe.** Some kids just don't fit in, and it's obvious. Some fit in too well, and that's obvious as well. Then there are those kids who are just hanging on, and no one seems to notice them.

Do these three things to build relationships with those on the fringe: 1. Make a special list of their names and pray for them everyday for six months. 2. If you are married, invite each teen over to your house to have supper. If you're not married, invite out two fringe kids at a time to supper at a restaurant. 3. Use some of your leaders to build relationships. Have each leader adopt at least one fringe kid to call weekly and give him or her special attention.

5 **Build relationships with parents who don't want to get involved in your ministry.** Here are three things you can do for parents who don't want to get involved: 1. Keep them informed of what's going on. They may spot something that piques their interest. 2. Write them a personal note once a month to encourage or praise their child. 3. Speak to them in person every chance you get. Never let a parent's uninvolvement be because they think you don't like him or her.

6 **Never cause conflicts between parents and teens.** Conflicts may come because of scheduling, but don't let it come from you personally. A danger in ministry is that teens may listen to you more than their parents. Never give advice contrary to a parent's. Never take sides. And never put down a parent in front of their children. Resolve all differences in private.

7 Accept teens where they are and move them toward Christ. Oh, how we long for a group of Davids ready to take on the world's Goliaths. But truth be known, some of the Goliaths are in the group. God rarely began with the great to accomplish His will. Moses, Jeremiah, Peter and others prove that. Be patient with each individual as they mature in Christ, and accept them for who they are and whose they are. Remember #3.

8 Spend time with teens individually. Group activities are great for the group, but not for those who need individual attention. Though it may not be possible to give each teen one on one time each month, here's a standard practice that probably will work for you.

Divide your group into thirds. Visit one third personally, call one third, and send a letter or card to the remaining third.

9 Attend events your teens are involved in (even if you don't want to). "He won't notice if I don't show up." Wrong. If a teen gives you a special invitation to come to a ball game, watch her cheer, or listen to a recital, go unless you absolutely can't. Get there early and talk with the student(s) before the performance. They will be thrilled you came and won't be hurt if you have to leave early. To be honest, teens attend a lot of things you invite them to, even if they don't want to (like devos), but don't you feel good when they do show up?

10 Create a diverse ministry. Most of us create a ministry around *our* talents. But because we are just one personality, everyone may not be ministered to through our means.

Create a diverse ministry by recognizing the needs of your kids and then reflect those needs in your ministry. Got some computer geeks? Help them create a ministry to reach their friends. Got some jock jerks? Their attitudes may quickly change when they get to reach out to their macho buddies through a Christian jock club.

Creating a diverse ministry will help you fulfill #1 in this book: Do whatever it takes to get teens to heaven.

GOD IS FOR LOSERS

We're all losers (Rom. 3:23)! That's why we need Jesus. It would take a real loser to give up all these benefits that Jesus brings (all from the book of Ephesians). So next time someone asks you, "What's so great about being a Christian?" or "What makes you different from anyone else?", you can show him!

1. **Eternal Life (God's prize) - Eph.1:14**
2. **Never alone (God's presence) - Eph. 3:16-17,19-20; 4:5-6**
3. **No fear (God's protection) - Eph.6:10-20**
4. **No worry (less pressure) - Eph. 3:20-21; 4:22-24**
5. **Salvation from sin (clean) - Eph. 1:7-8**
6. **Security (peace & comfort) - Eph. 1:2-3, 13-14; 2:14**
7. **God is our Father (relationship) - Eph. 1:5, 17; 3:6**
8. **Direction in life (absolutes) - Eph. 2:10; 4:24; 5:8-10, 15**
9. **Self-esteem (importance) - Eph.1:5, 11-14; 5:1-2, 8**
10. **Contentment (satisfaction) - Eph. 1:15-22; 4:28; 6:7**
11. **Joy (happiness) - Eph. 1:6,11,14; 5:18-20**
12. **Holy Spirit (empowerment) - Eph. 1:18-19; 3:16-21; 6:10-20**
13. **Providence of God (provision) - Eph. 1:3, 6; 6:11**
14. **Positive influence (example) - Eph. 4:20-5:7, 11; 6:19**
15. **Fellowship with others (family) - Eph. 2:11-22; 4:4**
16. **Love (of God & others) - Eph. 1:5; 2:4; 3:17-19; 4:2; 5:2**

THREE

hat Teens Look for Youth Minister

inister who:

I have needs. "I don't have time ...ted into "You are not important" by ...es teens want to talk. Sometimes ...g out. One way to be available is to ...u'll be at the office during the week ... Another way to be available is to tell ...r answering machine at home and that you will return calls as soon as you get their messages.

2 Has Jesus as the focal point of their life. Here's a quote to hang onto: "What you do reveals what you believe about God regardless of what you say" (from *Experiencing God*). Rate yourself, with #1 as "no focus," and #10 as "totally focused" on Jesus. Place your rating in this blank. _____

Let's be honest. Your group doesn't expect you to be perfect, but they do expect you to be authentic. And a genuine life dedicated to Christ will do more to mold the life of a young person than all youth conventions and lock-ins combined.

3 Is a great listener. When people have problems they often want an ear that listens, and not a lot of advice. Teens can work most of their difficulties out by talking about them. So don't just hear their words, listen with all of you by using these methods:

- Maintain eye contact.
- Nod (but don't nod-off) to show you understand where he or she is coming from.
- Keep your body loose. Folding your arms, or any other rigid position makes you look uninterested.

4 **Has a sense of humor.** Warning! This doesn't mean you have to try to be funny if you're not, just be fun to be around. Be able to laugh and cut up. Have the ability to smile when you can't pronounce a genealogy from Genesis. Most people are not stand up comics, but don't worry, you don't have to be one. Use your natural ability and the type of humor that God gave you.

5 **Is sympathetic and empathetic.** Basically, sympathy means you feel for someone. Empathy means you feel *with* someone. Either way it translates into, "I'm here for you." Use your life experiences to empathize. Use your heart experiences to sympathize.

6 **Is concerned about their salvation.** Use questions like, "How's your walk with God?" "What can I be praying about for you?" "Would you like to get together some time, get in the Word, and see how well you're growing in Christ?"

7 **Is competent.** No offense to a good friend of mine, but leaving the matches, plates, and buns for the wiener roast did not endear him to the group. Running out of gas on the way to the retreat didn't go over too well either. And forgetting a teen's name will never help himrank high on the competence level.

Ministry is a job that requires responsibility. Occasional mishaps are acceptable, but regular mistakes caused by lack of thinking are rarely soon forgotten.

8 **Is firm, but not overbearing.** No teen wants a drill sergeant for a youth minister. Be flexible enough to know when to let things slide, and when to crack the whip a bit.

Hebrews 12 talks about the discipline of

the Lord. Follow His example. He knows how to correct our sin without forcing us out of the kingdom. He knows when we need a gentle tug on the heart, or the rebuke of a friend. Be firm, without being rigid. Be strong, without being stiff. Be like Jesus.

"I want to know that my youth minister cares for me, and will be there for me no matter what."
- Amy, age 14

9 **Is willing to try new ideas.** Does this year's activities on the calendar look like a repeat of last year's? You may not feel like coming up with a list of new stuff, so let the teens do it. Take a survey of your group and have each person put down three things they would like your group to do that it has never done before. You will have plenty of options. From the expensive "Take a mission trip to Hawaii," to the wild "Host a wrestle mania," to the encouraging "Let's invite some needy families to our youth room for Christmas lunch."

10 **Expects and demands that teens succeed.** Create a spirit of excellence in your group. Colossians 3:17 says, "Whatever you do in word or deed do all to the glory of God..." Expect your teens to study, present devotionals, participate in class, etc. as if they were doing it directly for God.

Most people write young people off and think they are lazy and don't want to do anything. But the truth is they are willing to work as hard as anyone as long as they know it will be appreciated, and as long as they know you expect and demand the best they can offer.

FOUR

10 Tips for Building Credibility with Parents

1 **Let parents know you care.** Let them know that you are willing to do whatever it takes to get their teens to heaven. Don't just tell them you care, show them. Plan quarterly meetings that keep them up to date on the present ministry and what will be happening over the next few months. Check the copyright information, and make copies of any articles you think will help make their job easier, then pop them in the mail. Plan a PAN (Parents Appreciation Night) to honor parents.

2 **Provide parenting classes or workshops.** This will help you create a family ministry and prove that you are interested in the adult side of youth ministry as well. Of course, an excellent resource would be *Parents & Teens: Building Our Relationships Together*, available soon from Teen Life (for more information look in the back of this book).

3 **Schedule a Family Retreat.** Build credibility by building families. Few families today have enough time to get together regularly. Even fewer have the money to take a vacation together. Plan a Friday through Sunday retreat that will be inexpensive for families. Develop a family oriented theme, but keep a relaxed atmosphere that will provide plenty of time for parents and teens to explore, pray, and play together.

4 Attend events that their children are involved in. Although this was mentioned earlier from the teen perspective, parents will notice as well when you show up at their teen's play, or basketball game.

Spot as many parents as possible in the crowd and make an effort to speak to them. You might think that working a room is only for business professionals. But they're no fools, they know that the more hands they shake and the more sincere compliments they give will help make a positive lasting impression.

5 Use the telephone. Keep a list at your house and call parents just to see how they are doing. Ask if there is anything you can do that would help them as a parent. It will be a pleasant surprise that you are not calling to report misbehavior on the part of their child.

Designate 15 minutes three nights a week for these calls. You will be amazed at how many parents you can contact in 15 minutes. You will also be amazed at the level of friendship and trust you build as a result of these calls.

6 Send birthday cards. By the time you are an adult people rarely remember your birthday (maybe you don't want them to). The church office should have a record of members' birthdays. If not, send an information card to each family for them to fill out. This way you can make sure you have up to date addresses, email, telephone numbers, and birthdays. Mark all birthdays on your calendar and send a card a few days before. If you have the ability, send a homemade card designed especially for that particular parent.

7 Visit parents at home. Make an appointment to visit with the entire family. Ask about their dreams for the ministry and goals they may have. Ask about the ministry areas they feel have been successful.

In their homes, parents don't feel pressured or intimidated - like asking to see them in your office. This open atmosphere will allow you and the parents to be yourselves.

8 **Praise your parents and teens.** Take every opportunity to brag publicly on your families. Parents love to hear their child's name mentioned for something they accomplished. Parents may act embarrassed, but they like it too when they are mentioned for having such wonderful children.

Notice something special in each teen and then give the parents credit for it in private. If you notice that Julie always says "Yes, sir," and "Yes, ma'am" let the parents get some praise. Say, "I notice Julie always treats adults with respect by saying 'Yes, sir,' and 'Yes, ma'am.' I want to thank you for raising your child with manners."

> *Special tip: Always be sincere in your praise with parents and teens. These ten tips will help you build credibility only if they are genuine and from pure motives.*

9 **Involve parents in special ways.** Use a military parent for a war testimony when your class is on spiritual warfare. Bring in an accounting parent to show how God erases liabilities, and counts only assets. Allow them to use their experiences as a way to make Scripture real and interesting.

10 **Form parent support groups.** Parents can feel like they are facing their problems alone. They may feel like the only one facing a certain dilemma. Support groups help everyone involved realize that every parent struggles with some aspect of raising teenagers.

You may want to begin by asking a parent to facilitate the group for six weeks to determine how deep the need is in your congregation. Also, encourage the facilitator to provide open sharing. Parents may not be searching for answers as much as an empathetic ear.

FIVE

10 ? for a Personal Spiritual Checkup

1 How much time, or how often, do I pray each day? As ministers we spend a lot time time talking to others. Do we spend a lot of time talking to God? Do you spend seconds, minutes, or hours talking to God daily? Fill in the blank with your answer.___________

It may be that you don't keep up with the amount of time, but the number of times. So how often to do you pray? Place an "x" in the blank that fits you. ___ less than once a day. ___ Once a day. ___ Two or three times a day. ___Four to six times a day. ___ I feel like I am in a continual prayer with God.

2 How much time am I spending in God's Word? Forget it. Studying for lessons doesn't count unless you are purposely seeking a deeper walk with God from those studies.

Nothing can substitute for time alone with God. Use the margin to write down what your last personal Bible study was about, and how you grew from it.

3 How many people am I currently trying to win for Jesus? Write their names here .___________________

____

Jesus made it obvious that He came to seek and save the lost. As followers of Jesus we can do no less. Stay spiritually healthy by helping others come to know the Great Physician and receive His healing.

4 What is my favorite soul-winning memory? Part of staying in shape is remembering what it felt like, and remembering what you did when you were in your best shape. What feels better than knowing someone came to Jesus because of God's effort through you?

Use the margin and write a few notes about a favorite conversion memory. Was it with the kid that decided to accept Christ at an extinguished bonfire at 4 a.m.? Was it baptizing a new believer in the middle of January in Lake Winnotonga? Keep in touch with those special moments to keep you motivated in the present.

5 What does Christ and His church mean to me? Get a sheet of paper and take about thirty minutes for this question. Reread the crucifixion story. Read I Corinthians 12 about the body of Christ and let every positive thought about Christ and His bride flow out of your heart and onto the paper.

6 How often do I pray for and make positive comments about my church leaders? ________________
Every minister is in a different situation, but who hasn't gotten frustrated with the leaders at some point? You think you might get praised, but you garnish ridicule. You were sure this was the year for the raise, and it never surfaced in the budget meeting.

Stop right now and pray for your leaders. Pray for their wisdom and your understanding. Ask God to continue to work through those present in leadership as well as raise up new leaders who will extend the kingdom.

7 How deep is my relationship with God? Are you just staying afloat, or searching the spiritual depths? This is more of an intimacy question than a knowledge question. Some people know a lot *about* God, but don't *know* God. Shade in the spiritual depth finder to the right from top to bottom to establish where you feel you are spiritually. Later in the book you'll get 10 ways to go deeper with God.

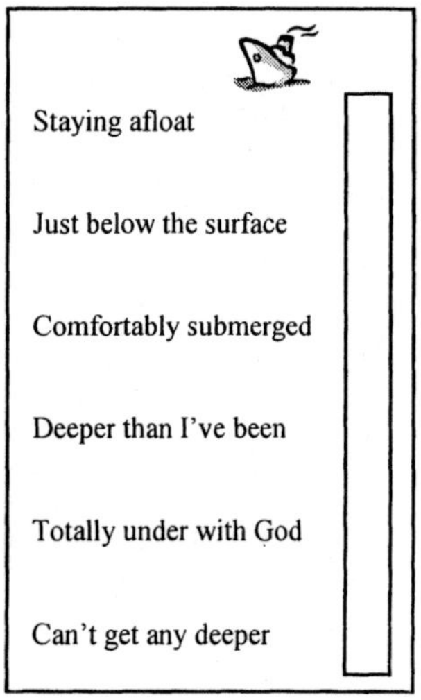

8 How much effort do I exert in helping teens lead their friends to Christ? ____________________
Providing tools for teens to evangelize is another way you may indirectly lead someone to Jesus. Create a sense of urgency in your group about the lost. We need to guard against a "take them or leave them" attitude. Again, the Lord came to "seek" the lost. The lost didn't just stumble onto the Savior, He went looking for them. Do the same with the teens in your group.

9 How often do I make excuses for not doing what I am called to do? Moses really didn't want the job. And he learned how to lose an argument with God very quickly. Yet we tend to follow his lead. Are you reluctant to follow when the Lord calls?

What is the last thing you knew God wanted you to do, but you offered an excuse?____________________

____

What excuse did you use? ____________________

____

What have you learned? ____________________

____

10 How often do I take a sabbatical, or spiritual retreat alone? Mark 1 gives us a day in the life of Jesus. He taught and healed the people. What do you think He did the next morning? Did He get up ready for another hard day? Did He wait at the door step for the praise of the people? Verse 35 reads, "Very early in the morning, while it was still dark, Jesus got up, left the house and when off to a solitary place, where he prayed."

Since our Lord knew the value of time alone with God, shouldn't we? When was the last date of your private spiritual retreat or sabbatical? ____________________
If it has been a while or not at all, start making plans today.

Well, how did you do? This isn't a pass or fail check-up, but maybe it will help make you aware of your spiritual position.

SIX

10 Techniques to Promote Class Discussion

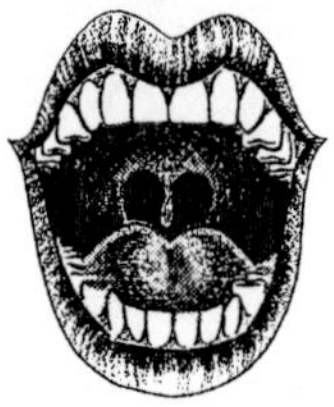

1 **Make sure the subject is relevant.** A class on The Christian Symbolism in World War II might be of some interest (maybe) to someone in your church, but not to teens. Stay on top of youth culture and create classes that meet teens where they are.

Teens might tire of hearing about sex and drugs, but the subjects will always be relevant. Other subjects may reveal themselves as a teachable moment, such as a classmate's untimely death.

2 **When asking questions, call on students by name to answer.** No teen wants to give a wrong answer, so few in class may volunteer an answer with risk on the line. But when a person is called by name, he or she feels obligated to give a response.

Instead of asking, "Who can tell me why Jesus is special to you?" turn it into a statement, "Lucy, tell us why Jesus is special to you."

3 **Grab Bag.** Put questions in a bag relevant to the topic and pass it around around the room. Have each student choose one question to discuss. Two general rules:
1) Make sure each student receives full class attention.
2) Never make fun of an answer.

Tip: Make the questions easy, but never answerable with "yes" or "no." Design them so a wrong answer is almost impossible.

4 Use real-life situations for illustrations. God formed the world so everything would point back to Him. That means almost any situation can hold spiritual significance. Keep your illustration antenna extended to pick up any usable situations. Write down anything that happens to you that you may be able to use later.

Read Ken Davis' book, *Secrets of Dynamic Communication,* to learn great ways to locate and use illustrations.

5 Tell stories. This differs from illustrations in that they are longer, and filled with details. Around Christmas time read a chapter to the class from a Max Lucado book. Rework parables so they have modern characters and language. Share short stories from various books.

Stories promote class discussion by first gaining the classes' interest, and then by allowing them to talk about something they just heard, not something taught six weeks ago.

6 Get Visual. Don't panic. We're not talking about a flannelgraph. Have a fireman come to devotional dressed in his uniform. Have him talk about the importance of each piece of equipment. Then say, "God protects us from Satan the way this gear protects the fireman from the flames. John, point out a piece of equipment and share God's version if it and how it protects His children." People are always more willing to talk about what they see than what they are asked to assume.

7 Bring in resource people. Another way to promote class discussion is to take the class to the moon - no, not literally, though you might want to send a few. Bring in people who are different from anything they have ever experienced.

Invite a blind individual to come and teach class on how God is the light of the world. When the circus comes to town ask the lion tamer to tell about the risks and rewards of training the big cats. These classes are great for students to get to ask questions and stimulating learning based on where they want to take the discussion.

8 **Play a tune.** What music is popular right now? What CD does every teen in your group own? Play the songs in class, supply a copy of lyrics, break the class into the groups, let them decipher the message of the song and any spiritual connotation. Select a group leader and ask him or her to share their group's findings.

Another option would be to take them to the moon again. Play some music from your youth and let teens compare it to their music today. Take them to Venus by playing some of your parent's music, your music, and their music for the ultimate comparison. If nothing else, they'll leave talking about how old you are.

9 **Be able to change approaches in mid-stream.** Part of promoting class discussion is flexibility. If a teen heads off on a tangent consider following it instead of pulling in the reins and getting the class back on your road. If everyone seems interested in the new topic let it ride to see what might be discovered.

10 **Keep learning!** The more you learn the more you realize how little you know. Here are three *must reads* to keep you abreast of ways to keep discussion flowing.

① *Color Outside the Lines* by Howard G. Hendricks

② *How to Speak to Youth and Keep Them Awake at the Same Time* by Ken Davis

③ *Ordinary Teachers, Extraordinary Results* by Michael D. Warden

SEVEN

10 Frustrations of Youth Ministry

1 **Losing teens.** Whether to the world, another group, or relocation, losing a teen pulls a minister down. And it always seems to happen when the kid was making a breakthrough, or having a tremendous impact on the rest of the group.

Tip: Don't take it personally when a teen leaves. It may be her parent's decision. Or he may not have fit in well with the dynamics of your group and decided to try another group. Instead of being hard on yourself, pray and ask God to bless the teen wherever he or she may go.

2 **Lack of Commitment.** "How many want to get together and pray before school at your campus?...No one?..Okay, then how many would be interested in hosting a free car wash next month for the senior citizens? ... Anyone?... No?...Okay, then how about..." In youth ministry cycles there come periods when no one acts like they want to do anything for the Lord. Casual Christianity seems to rule.

Tip: When no one wants to get involved, have the teens plan, and host the event. By giving them ownership, they put in the time and energy. Teens might not mind if your plans don't work, but they will if their plans don't work.

3 **Poor Attendance.** I remember showing up one Saturday morning to go with my youth group to a rally. Only the youth minister showed up out of a group with seventy

teens. Do you know what my youth minister did? He took me to the rally!

Tip: Don't worry about poor attendance. View it as an opportunity to give special attention to the handful that do show up.

4 **Lack of Parental Support.** Even if you do everything you can to get parents on your side, there may be times when you lack the support you desire and need. As the youth minister, you may get blamed for a teen's personal problems because, "You didn't do enough." Or you may not be going in the direction that the parents want you to.

Tip: Regardless of the circumstances, avoid overreacting. Treat parents with respect and honor through the hard times and the next time things get rough you may find that you have more supporters than ever before.

5 **Lack of Staff Member Support.** Even if the parents aren't on your side all the time, you certainly want the staff on your side. These are the people you work with everyday - they're hard to avoid!

Tip: Tensions on staff arise from multiple sources: envy, personality, salary, office hours, to name a few. Keep relationships strong by having a weekly share session to talk about problems, prayer requests, and dreams. Form a team concept among staff members.

6 **Not enough time.** There are only twenty-four hours in a day, and nothing will change that. You put in your office time, visit with kids after school, catch a quick supper, and then attend a school function of one of the teens. This cycle can seem endless when you suddenly realize you have to get a class, devotional, and leader's material ready by this afternoon!

Tip: Prioritize your time. There never seems to be enough time when you don't know what's coming next. Review your day each morning and make every minute count.

7 **Unjustified Complaints.** We're human and we're going to make mistakes. Truth be known, I make a lot of mistakes. That's why I don't like getting the blame for

something I had nothing to do with.

Tip: Consider the source. Does the complainer have the right information, the right attitude, and the right credentials to bring the complaint? Consider the nature of the complaint. Is there any truth in it. Finally, offer a solution if the complaint has some validity. Forget about it if it doesn't.

8 **Low Budget.** Keep fighting in this department. It can be a never-ending battle. Read "Low Cost, No Cost Ideas" by *Group* for a mass of ideas.

Tip: Make a list of youth group alumni and ask them to contribute five or ten dollars a month to the youth fund. Ask them to sign up for a year at the time. You'll be amazed at the number of people willing to do this when they have been blessed by the ministry in the past.

9 **Cliques in the group.** Before getting too concerned, make sure cliques really exist. A clique happens when subgroups form to the exclusion of others. Do your teens try purposely to leave others out, or are they just being thoughtless?

Tip: If cliques do exist, put everyone in a seating arrangement next to someone they are not close to and tell them they can't sit where they want until the cliques disappear (just kidding). Of more benefit may be using small groups in class where students draw names each time to see who they are paired with. That way they get to work with people they are close to and get to know others at the same time.

10 **Undisciplined Teens.** Some teens won't listen or behave. They try to make you look like a fool in front of the group.

Tip: Love'em anyway. Deal with the troublemakers with patience and pray that your seeds of love will bring a harvest.

EIGHT

10 Tips for Recruiting Volunteers

1 Don't wait till the last minute. Begin early with your recruiting for several reasons. Most adult volunteers have full time jobs so they need to know in advance if time off from work will be required. If you wait until the last minute those who assist you may feel rushed to make the decision, or they may feel unprepared to do a good job. Also, if you wait till the last minute the person you think would be best for the position may already be assigned by another ministry. Look over next year's schedule and mark the events that need volunteer assistance and start recruiting now.

2 Recruit in person. It's a poor idea to ask for ministry volunteers with a general plea from the pulpit unless you want a lot of "generals" in your ministry. Typically, unqualified people sign up when it's open to everyone, which can result in an embarrassment to the person, the ministry, and yourself.

Make a list of prime candidates and solicit them in person. By hand picking volunteers, you ensure getting the ones you feel are best for the job.

3 Provide adequate answer time. Give volunteers at least a week to pray and think about the role you are asking of them before they have to make the decision. Never push for a quick answer.

4 **Be up front.** Let your volunteers know what you expect from them even before their ministry begins. Let them know how much time and energy it will require, what their job will entail, and how you expect excellence. Volunteers may quickly feel overwhelmed, or ineffective if they don't know exactly what to do. You don't have to hold their hands, but do hold their hearts.

5 **Let volunteers help develop their ministry role.** Point your volunteer in the direction you want him or her to go, then ask that they share their vision for the ministry. Give them hands on experience in designing and growing their portion of the ministry by allowing them to submit their ideas to you and take risks.. It's a fact that people are more committed and do a better job when they share ownership.

6 **Let volunteers know they are not alone.** Volunteers need the assurance that they will not be in for a struggle alone. Offer your support and guidance from the moment they accept responsibility. Provide your home phone number to let volunteers know you are available for them at all hours.

7 **Check in, but don't check up.** Call all volunteers once a week to make sure everything is going well in their ministry, and reassure them of #6. Use questions that probe for any help they may need, such as: "Is there anything I can do from my end to help your ministry?" or "How are you dong spiritually?"

Avoid using language or questions that indicate you are unsure about the job they are doing. Such as: "Are you sure you don't need some help? This project really needs to go well."

8 **Demand an uncompromised lifestyle.** Enlist volunteers who are talented, motivated, and joyful, but most of all godly. The biblical precedents set for leaders go for volunteers as well.

Create your own commitment contract for your volunteers based on your church's tradition, and expect your volunteers to sign it before they can go into action. Here are a few things that should be on your list no matter what your fellowship:

- Jesus is the Lord and Savior of my life.
- I refuse to participate in gossip.
- I will always uphold the values of this ministry.
- I will love each teen without partiality.
- I will commit for ________(length of time).

Spend an afternoon writing your volunteer contracts. A contract helps the volunteer know the expectations that come with the position, and will serve as a constant reminder of the oath associated with their ministry.

9 **Praise Privately.** Don't just catch volunteers doing something right, catch them doing lots of things right. Keep a stack of thank you cards handy to send when you witness or hear about a volunteer's good work. Keep a set of postcards nearby as well to send during the week as thoughts of encouragement. Place a sticky note on their car door that simply says "Thank you" and don't sign it. Pour on the praise without reservation in as many ways as possible.

10 **Praise Publicly.** Once a year hold a volunteer appreciation banquet to honor all your ministry servants. If your church prints a bulletin or service sheet, publish the names of all volunteers along with their area of service. If you can, bring them on stage during a service so the entire congregation can thank them.

Praising publicly not only helps you hold on to the volunteers you have, it helps you recruit. Who wouldn't want to become part of a ministry where they are actually appreciated?

NINE

10 Time Management Tips

1 **Begin each day and project with prayer.** Instead of thinking about managing your time, think about it as managing *God's* time. Ask for His wisdom during decision- making. Ask for His insight when studying and preparing for classes and lessons. Make I Thessalonians 5:22 your creed and pray without ceasing. It will give meaning to every minute.

2 **Keep a Day-Timer.** It's hard to manage time when you don't know where it's going next. The Moody Bible Institute's Life System is an excellent resource (1-800-600-LIFE).

Use a two page daily system to have plenty of room for notes, goals and "to do" items. As you make your list, prioritize by placing an "A", "B", or "C" next to each activity. Check off or draw a line through each one as they are accomplished. At the end of the day you will be able to review your accomplishments and know you used God's time wisely.

3 **Acquire Discipline.** How many times have you started a project only to get side-tracked by someone or something else? Discipline yourself to stay with the task at hand until it is complete. While some interruptions are unavoidable, others come as a result of being easily

diverted.

4 **Handle the toughest job first.** As you look at your prioritized list, go ahead and prioritize all the "A's" on it. Number them 1 to 5 in order of importance, and knock out the most critical while you are fresh. Whether this first job is physically or mentally demanding, getting it out of the way will still give you plenty of resolve for the rest of the items that won't require as much energy.

> *Instead of thinking about managing your time, think about it as managing God's time.*

5 **Take regular breaks.** As a general rule take a ten minute break every two hours. Walk around the building. Take a walk outside. Go in one direction for five minutes then turn and return.

Working without breaks does not mean you will accomplish more. Mental fatigue from too many computer hours or prolonged study will lessen mental sharpness and increase mistakes. This translates into having to do the same job twice when it could have been done right the first time.

6 **Use time twice.** Do two things at once to save time. If you have a stack of letters to stuff in envelopes, do it while brainstorming with a staff member about an upcoming event. Listen to motivational tapes while you clean your office. Watch a video series while relaxing. Memorize scriptures as you drive to work.

7 **Purposely plan uninterrupted time.** For tasks that involve complete focus, tell the secretary to hold all calls or turn on the church answering machine. Let staff members know not to disturb you for "x" amount of time.

If possible get out of the office. Go to the library to study, or a classroom away from the office. Blocking time without interruptions does not paint you as unsociable, but focused. There will be plenty of interruptions in the days ahead, don't feel guilty for taking this time.

8 **Establish health habits.** It's no secret that people are more productive when they eat and exercise properly. Proper diet will enhance mental capabilities and keep you focused. Getting seven or more hours of sleep each night will result in more productivity. What? There's no way you can get that much sleep? It's impossible to eat well when all teens want is pizza? You're too exhausted to exercise?

Put sleep down as an "A" priority and go to bed at a reasonable hour. You don't have to give up pizza, but you can limit yourself to a couple of pieces. And you can do light exercise during your breaks. Actually, we make time for what we want to do. Put health at the top of the list of goals if want to manage God's time well.

9 **Delegate** (n. - a person authorized to act for others). What are you doing that someone else could do for you? Need to make twenty youth song books? Perhaps you have three teens who would do a good job of putting them together. Not only does delegating work take pressure off of you and allow you to use time somewhere else, it provides others an opportunity to serve and get involved in ministry.

10 **Let technology work for you.** If every member of the group needs to get an urgent message, use email. Keep a database updated so you can print labels instead of hand-addressing each mailing. Acquire a machine or computer program that will call all teens and parents and give them a message you recorded. Call bookstores, etc. before you ride over to see if they have what you want and discover that it will have to be special ordered.

10 Tools for Boosting Creativity

1 **Exercise your brain.** The "use it or lose it" rule applies to the brain as well as other parts of the body. Most people feel they are creative or they are not, and that's just the way it is. Not so. Those who are naturally creative can lose that spark if they fail to keep it fresh within them. A person who is very analytical can become creative by training himself.

Two of the easiest ways to exercise your brain into greater creativity is through reading and writing. Both are brain stimulants that require visualization and imagination to form a reality within our minds. Think about the parable of the sower. Can you see him tossing his seed? Can you smell the dry earth as he walks? As you picture it in your mind write it down. From the page let the words become pictures in your mind, then from your mind to another page let the pictures become words again.

2 **Brainstorm.** Whether as an individual or in a group, this is a fantastic way to get your brain creatively charged. Take out a sheet of paper and write your subject at the top. For example, you want to do a lesson on the birth of Jesus. Give yourself ten minutes to write down as many words or phrases as you can that match the theme. (Angels, shepherds, Simeon, cattle, sheep, lamps, inn, stable...) Don't worry about a certain direction, just list.

Brainstorming will allow you to write down everything that comes to mind and may cause you to approach the subject from a different angle than before.

3 **Take a walk in a mental park.** If you are feeling particularly uncreative, take a mental walk in the park. See the man in the ragged coat feeding bread crumbs to the pigeons? Stare at your reflection in the wishing well. How many pennies can you count? Smell the tulips. Feel the breeze. This type of exercise gives your brain permission to step outside its usual stuffiness.

4 **Limit television.** The rapid fire video of television, video tapes, movies, etc. dulls our perception and numbs our thinking. Unfiltered television can leave you feeling depressed and lethargic. Be discriminating in what you watch. Watch motivating speakers and view movies that end in triumph. Stay away from any program that isn't what Christ would watch if you want your creativity and purity to remain high.

5 **Listen to soft music.** Studies confirm that classical music, ballads and the like produce far more creativity than harder music. Why? Because our brains function best when relaxed rather than when tensed. Choose music that relaxes and frees you from tension.

6 **Keep a recorder or small note pad with you at all times.** Chances are you have thought of several "great" ideas only to lose them seconds later. Part of being creative is using common sense. We forget where we put our keys, or if we turned off the stove. It's natural that we would forget a super idea, so write it down or record it on the spot. That way you won't be tempted to jot it down as soon as you get to the...now where was I going with this?

7 **Use reference tools.** Creativity doesn't mean originality. Part of being creative is to use what exists and take it to the next level, or use it in a different way. Let's go back to the birth of Jesus lesson we were talking about earlier. Get a stack of magazines and thumb

through them. Answer this question. Where would Jesus be born if He came today? You flip pages and spot an upper dollar hotel. *That doesn't seem right.* You keep flipping and notice a row of cardboard shanty houses. *Hmmm, nah.* Then you notice a picture of Central Park in New York. *Maybe so.* Use magazines, books, dictionaries, whatever you find to spur your mind into seeing a different angle.

8 **Spend an unpredictable day regularly.** Another reason we have difficulty being creative is we are so predictable. We tend to think the same way on a daily basis. We eat the same foods and drive the same way to work.

Take an occasional day and be different. Take a different route to work. Eat something new at lunch. Do this and you will confound your friends and find that you are thinking and noticing things you have been missing.

9 **Get adequate mental and physical rest.** We've already touched on this, so allow me to repeat two things. First, take a ten minute break every two hours. Second, get seven to eight hours of sleep each night.

10 **Spend time with creative people.** List three people in the margin right now whom you consider creative. Get on the phone and invite him or her to lunch to listen and learn.

Haven't you been around people who are positive and you left their presence feeling positive as well? Why? Because we become like who we are around. We become like our focus. The more creative people you surround yourself with, the more creative you will become.

Eleven

10 Reasons Teens Leave the Church

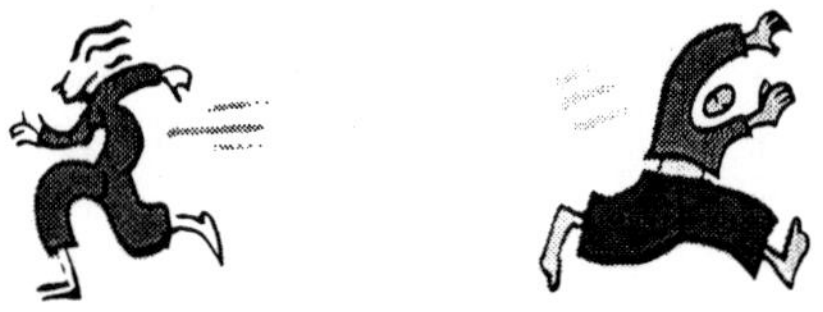

1 **Never converted.** When a person grows up going to church, it's easy to adopt a belief system without owning it. Verses may get memorized, but not internalized. Confession may be made, but not a commitment.

When teens graduate from high school they often graduate from church as well. Prevent it by helping teens develop a personal faith. A faith in Christ, not the church. A faith in God, not in an earthly person.

2 **They hear their parents say one thing, but see them do another.** When talking about the Pharisees, Jesus said, "Do what they say, but not what they do, because they say and do not." Just like Jesus, teens hate a fake. Teens do not think it's fair for their parents to expect one standard from them, yet refuse to live up to that same standard in their own lives. It says to them that Christianity is more about talk than life. So when they leave home, they leave the talk and life behind as well.

3 **Teens rarely get an opportunity to do the work of the church.** The youth group is a special place, but teens know it's often viewed as a separate area of the church filled with "kids." They hear about being the "future of the church," and seldom get to be the church of today.

Let teens be part of your entire congregation by using them to help teach children's classes, help in the nursery and other areas, to allow the "adults" to see them at work. These responsibilities may seem "small" to the teens, but will form a great impression on those around them and help them be considered for greater responsibilities.

4. Problems. Teens are good at sharing their victories, but poor at sharing their problems. They play cover-up Christianity in an effort to appear all together. When problems become overwhelming and they feel they can't live up to expectations, bailing out seems easier than fessing up.

Foster openness in your group by providing classes, devotionals, etc. expressly for problem sharing. Share some of your own struggles as well. You won't appear weak, rather teens will be able to relate to you and the group better when they know everyone has problems.

5. Hurt by the church. We could all make a list as long as our leg of people who left the church because they got "offended." Teens are no different. Offend or hurt their feelings and they leave. Hopefully they will go to another church, most likely they won't go at all, and their parents won't blame them.

When you feel justified in smarting off or pinching the feelings of a teen to "teach them a lesson," remember Romans 15:1. "We who are strong ought to bear the failings of the weak and not to please ourselves."

> *When a teen leaves the church, interview him or her. Ask for their blatant honesty in telling you fully about the reason(s) for leaving.*

6. Peer pressure. Part, if not most, of the reason a teenager becomes part of a certain church is friendship. Teens go where the crowd goes. Teens do what their friends do. And if a majority of their friends don't go to church, they'll probably dodge it every chance they get if they are not committed to Jesus.

Protect your group by promoting positive peer pressure. Encourage friendships among Christians, while evangelizing their non-Christian friends.

7 **Negative influences.** "Do not be misled: Bad company corrupts good character," I Corinthians 15:33. This not only applies to negative peer pressure, but television, movies, books, magazines, and anything else that's "bad company."

One of the most dangerous influences today is the internet. Teens can click their way into any kind of sin imaginable. And when sin defeats, teens either repent or give up.

8 **Church member hypocrisy.** You've probably heard about the guy who refused to go to church because of the hypocrites. His friend told him, "Awe, come on. You can go with me. There's always room for one more."

Teens use hypocrisy as an excuse rather than a true reason for leaving the church. Typically they have been hurt, or lack commitment. In reality, they know there is no place on earth they can go without finding hypocrites.

9 **Low self-image.** When teens don't like themselves, they find it hard to imagine that anyone else likes them. *How can God love me when I don't like me?*

Have teens with a low self-image memorize Psalm 139:14, "I praise you because I am fearfully and wonderfully made; your works are wonderful, I know that full well." Take teens to a garden and point to the flowers. Let them comment on the beauty of God's creation, then have them read the Psalm or quote it. It may not take away all their insecurities, but it will help them see what God means by this verse and how special they are to Him.

10 **Too much time and effort.** Just a few months ago I heard a long time believer say, "Christianity is too hard. It's not worth everything I have to give up." Don't teens think the same way? Don't we all tend to concentrate on what we give up, rather than what we gain in Christ?

Urge teens who are struggling with the effort required to live for Christ to understand that everyone struggles (Romans 7), but that the reward in Jesus far surpasses anything we could gain here on earth (Philippians 3:1-14).

TWELVE

10 Tips for Teaching Teens

1 Teach, don't preach. Preaching tells teens what to think. Teaching allows teens to discover it for themselves. Another way to put that is: Teens *might* believe what you tell them, they *will* believe what they tell themselves.

2 Know your teens. Your class is made up of several personalities. Some just want the facts. Some want to think about a point for days before adopting it. Others stay confused, while some want to have fun. Learn the different personalities in your class and design the lessons in such a way that each person will walk out with one thing to concentrate on. Teaching according to the make up of your class is crucial to success.

3 Concentrate on one thing at a time. One thought. One theme. One over all point. Let every illustration, joke, class exercise, etc. tie directly into the theme for the day. Resist the urge to throw something in because it's cute. It doesn't refer to the theme, leave it out. If you have one theme, you are likely to hit the target in the bullseye. If you try to tie several topics together, you run the risk of teens leaving unsure of anything you attempted to teach.

Know your topic. School teachers are required to produce lessons plans as part of their preparation for class. What does that mean to you and me? We need to plan our lessons. "Winging it" might work occasionally, but it will catch up with you. Block out a regular time each week for study and class preparation.

4 Ask & build. Use questions to open the door of discovery, then build on what the teens reveal. For example, in teaching from John 4:24-25, Jesus says God is looking for what kind of worshippers? Answer from the class: "Those who worship in spirit and truth." Now build off their answer. What are four ways to worship in spirit and truth? List their suggestions, which may include singing, serving, prayer, and praise. Build again by worshipping on the spot using one of the methods the class listed.

5 Use short series. Keep the interest of your group by working through a series. Study the Holy Spirit for a month. Study the book of James in five weeks.

Draw interest by developing clever titles. One I will never forget was mentioned by Rick Warren when teaching about the demon possessed man of Mark 5. He titled it, "A Nude Dude in a Rude Mood." Or how about a series on Jonah called, "You Can't Keep A Good Man Down."

6 Employ memory devices. Most of us grew up hearing about G.R.A.C.E.: God's Riches At Christ's Expense. That's hard to forget isn't it? Use the same technique in your classes to help teens remember. You can use an acrostic, or have your points start with the same letter such as a lesson on God: 1. Majestic 2. Mighty 3. Master. Or use the same beginning phrase: 1. God is love. 2. God is peace. 3. God is near. Ask this question when putting your lesson together, "How can I arrange this so it is unforgettable?"

7 Create an atmosphere. An area easily overlooked is the classroom. Does your meeting place look and feel academic? If so, you're risking retention. Decorate your room to reflect the people who will be in it. Give it a feeling of fun. From the moment teens walk in they need to be saying, "This is where I belong."

Select a youth team to redesign your room if needed. Develop the decor around a theme, or nick-name of your group.

8 Pray, pray, pray. Continually ask God for the words, illustrations, and points to use. Ask Him to let His words come out of your mouth. Pray for a creative spirit to construct classes that will be dynamic and unforgettable.

We treat prayer like a blanket for everything and use it almost casually for solutions. We shouldn't. When we pray we are asking God to do something that would not have occurred had we not asked. It is the movement of His power at His child's request. So throughout this book as we mention prayer it's not because it's an easy point, it's a critical necessity.

9 **Keep the class moving.** Switch activities, or presentation styles, every seven to ten minutes. Instead of starting with a video then lecturing for forty minutes use a rapid fire approach. 1. Begin with a testimony. 2. Divide into groups to discuss it. 3. Come together and study a passage relating to the first two items. 4. Show a ten minute video. 5. Ask questions from the video that will make the previous Bible passage come to life.

You can use any format you want just don't become predictably. Teens already think they know everything there's no need to prove it by being predictable.

10 **Evaluate each class.** Here are three ways to approach evaluation. First, you can simply take time the next day to relive the class or devotional. What went great? What went wrong? When did you seem to lose their attention? What worked that you didn't expect to? What flopped that you thought would fly? Why? What can be learned from last night?

Second, ask five teens to evaluate the class from their perspective. List ten questions like those above that you would like them to answer. This approach may seem brutal, but not as bad as number three.

Third, video tape your classes and watch them for your viewing displeasure. There is no better or quicker way to enhance your teaching than viewing it from the class perspective. The tape will not lie. Count the uuhh's, keep track of any repetitive physical habits. Notice your voice inflection, or lack of it.

Evaluate on one or all three of these methods and become a better teacher.

THIRTEEN

10 Tools for Bible Study

1 **A variety of versions.** Get the clearest meaning of a passage through the use of different versions. KJV, NIV, the Message; it's your choice, just don't limit yourself to a paraphrase. A translation (KJV, NIV) was written from the original language of the text and consists of numerous translators. A paraphrase is based on an existing version and is usually one man's interpretation of that version using modern terms.

2 **Concordances.** Strong's Concordances links words and topics to the King James version of the Bible. Other concordances are available for other versions.

Concordances give you every location of a word in the Word. Want to know every verse that contains the word miracle? Look it up in a concordance. It will give you the phrase of the verse and the reference. Most Bibles have a limited concordance in the back, but if you are interested in getting serious about Bible study, then purchase a full concordance.

3 **Dictionaries.** Several dictionaries can be helpful in study. A general one that is almost encyclopedic will give you not only definitions of words, but also the history and background of the word.

Hebrew and Greek dictionaries allow you to discover the original meaning of a text for yourself. If you are not a language scholar you will need a Hebrew Old Testament, and a Greek New Testament that provide the original word under the English word with it's corresponding linking number to look it up.

4 **Commentaries.** This tool gives you the insight and thoughts of a scholar or scholars. The NIV Study Bible contains an excellent commentary along with the text. If you are interested in a full volume commentary series, do your research before purchasing. Talk to several ministers in your area and gather their recommendations about various commentaries.

5 **Books on the subject.** Always begin and end with God's Word, but don't neglect the works of others. Suppose you are doing a series on the life of Joseph. Call your area Christian bookstore and ask them to run a search on Joseph. There may be some books worth purchasing, or ask if it would be alright for you to thumb through them to gather a few references.

6 **Other ministers.** There is no need to come up with all the information yourself; perhaps someone else has already done the work. Call your friends in ministry and ask for their input. Discover their approach on a subject.

Contact areas ministers whom you may not know well and gather their thoughts. Not only will you gain knowledge, but new friends as well.

P.S. Don't forget to ask your co-worker who happens to be located conveniently in your offices.

7 **Illustration and quote books.** After working so hard to harvest all this information, arrange it and make it pleasantly presentable. Illustrations and quotes do two things. First, they add credibility to your lesson. Second, they add color. "With the right illustration the most boring of facts bloom in the mind of the learner," says Paul Evans (see what I mean?)

8 **Software.** If you have a computer at your office, all of the above tools are available on CD-ROM. One of the most popular is QuickVerse. These point-and-click programs are easy to use and make it possible to line up your reference tools side by

side. Bible software is great because you can be studying Damascus and be taken instantly to a map, another click takes you to a dictionary, another takes you to other articles referenced by the article you are presently reading. If you're not careful, you'll have more than you'll ever use - isn't that great!

If you would like to save big bucks on software and books for study, call Christian Book Distributors at 1-978-977-5000, or online, www.christianbook.com.

9 **A note-pad and pencil.** With all this talk about study, you didn't think we'd let you walk away without writing it down, did you?

Before leaving your study area, organize your notes in some fashion in case you need to return and review a reference. Write down *anything* you think you might use.

10 **The right spot.** Find a favorite study location and go there frequently. Some youth ministers love the library, others go to a restaurant and spend an afternoon. Maybe under a tall oak on the back of the church property would suit you well. Wherever you choose to go, let it be a place that results in free thinking and expressiveness. Study tends to constrict our view, so decide on a place that leaves you feeling free from tension and distractions.

"You don't get a well-fed church from serving fast-food."
-- Bill Hybels

FOURTEEN

10 Tips for Staying Physically Healthy

1 **Get convicted.** Someone once told me years ago that we workout for two reasons. Either to live longer and serve God longer, or to live longer and serve Satan longer.

Whether we like the shape of it or not, God has chosen this fleshly frame to take the good news of Jesus to the world. The healthier it is the better we can accomplish God's will. And if that's not enough to convict you, please remember that our bodies house the Holy Spirit. (I Corinthian 6:19) Let's give Him a great place to live.

2 **Get a physical.** Ouch! This is another major reason for conviction. It's going to take some to get you in the doctor's office for a physical examination. Before beginning any diet or exercise routine, get thoroughly checked out by your physician. Your doctor will be able to recommend the type of program for you to begin with, considering your present level of health. He or she will also be able to make you aware of any risks to your health that you may not be aware of.

3 **Get a goal.** Do you need to gain weight or lose weight? Do you need to increase your cardiovascular fitness so you can take the teens on the basketball court? Write down your goals and make them specific. I want to lose _____pounds by this date_______, and I will do it through the following 1.__________, 2.___________, 3.__________

4 Get a plan. Your doctor may be able to suggest an exercise routine for you to follow. It will probably be general and good enough to get you in decent shape. At a minimum it will require thirty minutes, three times a week.

Another option is to join a local health club and have a licensed trainer design a specific routine based on your goals. Most quality clubs will offer this free of charge for new members.

More options include purchasing a book on the type of exercise you are interested in and following a program outlined in the pages. Finally, if you know some people in great shape, ask one of them to help you get started.

5 Get Consistent. When you have a plan in hand, stick with it. It takes four to six weeks to make enough physical changes for others to notice, so don't get discouraged after a week of stiff muscles and decide to give up.

Designate your workout times in your calendar and be consistent. Don't miss unless you have no choice. We expect teens who want to be spiritually strong to make a consistent commitment to the group. No less goes for your physical health.

6 Get a food conscience. Like cars, our bodies need fuel to function. The type of fuel does make a difference. When we eat foods that are pure, our bodies function correctly and we feel better. Whereas, if we fuel with junk food, the opposite is true. This doesn't mean you have to give up burgers and fries, especially if you have a high metabolism, just remain balanced in what you eat.

7 Get informed. Knowledge can help the task of staying consistent easier. Inform yourself on what is in the food you eat. When you discover that pigs feet and pigs ears are in those hot dogs, you might not eat as many. When you learn that the walk you just got back from burned 200 calories, and that peanut butter cup you want has 280 calories, chances are better you'll leave it in the wrapper.

8 **Get Smart.** Use the information you gain in a practical way. A gram of protein and a gram of carbohydrate both contain 4 calories. A gram of fat contains 9 calories. Get smart: you can eat more volume of protein and carbohydrate combined than fat. Get smart again: Not eating fat does not mean you won't get fat. If you only need 2000 calories a day to maintain your weight, eating more calories, whether from fat, protein, or carbohydrates, will make you gain weight. A good general rule for eating is to eat breakfast like a king, lunch like a prince and supper like a pauper.

9 **Get a journal.** Write down everything you consume and every exercise you do. Keeping a record will provide detailed proof of what works and what doesn't work for you. Notice the records around the holidays. OH! That's where those five pounds came from!

10 **Get a partner.** People who train together get fit together faster. Find someone on staff, or in the congregation who is willing to commit with you. It helps to have someone pushing you, and making sure you show up to get pushed.

Another option that will help your ministry is to get permission to train with the high school football team in the fall, the basketball team in the winter, and the baseball or track team in the spring. Use the time to get to know the teens in those sports and invite them to join your group and get to know Christ. By the end of one school year you'll know a lot of teenagers and be in great shape, or be worn out!

Get a Life. When you decide to begin a training regimen, do it for life. Make it your lifestyle and not something you do until you've gotten the body you want.

FIFTEEN

10 Counseling Techniques

1 **Reflecting.** Reflection is the process of restating to the teen what was stated to you. By reflecting you begin to understand where the teen is coming from and the teen begins to feel understood. A teen might say, "This has been the worst week of my life. I failed my tests at school. My parents are furious because I dented the car. And on top of that my girlfriend broke up with me." Reflection: "It sounds like you had a tough week with a lot of problems. I am so sorry." Teen: "I don't know where to begin." Reflection: "I can tell you're frustrated and are searching for answers."

2 **Interpreting.** Use sensitive terms in question form when placing meaning with a teen's words. Teen: "When I'm mad at my parents, I throw things or act like I'm going to hit them." Interpretation: "Do you think that your temper and acting out is a way to show your parents that you are in control?"

3 **Teaching.** This technique involves giving advice for the teen to follow. Teaching is used most frequently when counseling a teen who has difficulty formulating or gaining information on their own. Work with caution in all forms of counseling, but especially this one. Instead of leading a teen to make a decision for himself or herself, you are making the decision for them. Limit teaching in

your counseling practices.

4 Encouraging. Encouragement can make a teen feel wanted, needed and understood. One way to do this is to let them know they are not alone. Another is to let them know that the problem can be solved if they are willing to work on it. Be honest when using encouragement. Don't give out false hope, or say things that make teens believe their problems will drift away.

5 Probing. Probing comments can stimulate further discussion, particularly with teens who are bashful or quiet. Probing: "Tell me more about your family-life and what you are specifically wrestling with." "What are some areas of your life you need to work on?" "If you could do it over again how would you handle the situation differently?"

6 Self-disclosing. This technique allows you to draw from your personal experience to connect with a teen. It is common for a counselor to have faced a similar situation as the teen they are encountering. Self-disclosure: "I understand how you feel. I have gone through the same thing myself. Tell me if this situation sounds like yours." You may chose to verbalize your statement, or use your knowledge from past experience to guide the teen to a self-discovered solution. If you do decide to tell your experience, make sure the teen does not view this as approval of his or her behavior.

7 Listening. Silence is one of the most difficult techniques, especially if you have little counseling experience. It's good to employ silence when a teen has made a statement or answered a question. It permits the teen a moment to absorb their answer, or search for an answer on their own to the question they just asked.

Teen: "What's the first step is getting right with my parents?" Use silence and let the teen answer their own question. "Maybe, I ought to say I'm sorry first. They won't expect that."

8 Questioning. Use one question at a time when counseling and be sure it cannot be answered with "yes" or "no."

Questioning misapplied: “Your parents said you got in late last night, is that true?” Teen: “Yep.”

Questioning: “You’re parents mentioned that you got in late last night. Why?” Teen: “We lost track of time.” Questioning: “What were you doing that caused you to forget about curfew?”

9 Confronting. Confronting a teen will require that you have built a solid relationship and that they trust you completely knowing that you are looking out for their good. You are not trying to make a teen mad, but get them to be honest and forth right. Though the word confronting doesn’t sound so, you need to be compassionate, gentle and patient when using it.

Confronting: “You know Todd, I don’t want to hurt you, but you come in here each week and lie. If you are not going to be honest, there is no need for us to get together.” If the relationship is right, the teen will understand what you require and will conform.

10 Evaluating. This is done during and after each counseling session, whether consciously or unconsciously. In the above example, saying Todd was lying was based on evaluation. It’s what the counselor concludes, given the facts and circumstances.

Evaluation is subjective. Basically you give your advice or make a statement about the teen based on what you believe is the heart of the problem and all the techniques used to reveal it. Sometimes your evaluation leads to “This teen needs some attention.” And other times, “This teen needs to undergo a professional psychiatric evaluation.”

Most teens who show up for counseling only need someone to listen to them. If you are not a trained counselor, refer a teen to someone more helpful, especially if you feel the situation is beyond your ability.

SIXTEEN

10 All Time Great Service Projects

1 Cookout for city sanitation workers. Have you ever noticed those guys who ride around and pick up the trash on your curb? Have you ever thought they may not feel appreciated? In most cities the sanitation workers meet a couple of times a week for lunch in the area they're working. Call the city and ask where the sanitation workers in your area meet and on what days. Once you have this information, get your group together and plan a cookout for the workers. Make invitations and deliver them a week in advance. Go ahead and ask if they will come. Chances are good they won't turn down a free meal. When they arrive at the cookout, seat them, serve them, and clean up after them. The only thing they have to do is show up, eat, and be honored.

2 Bake and take. Meet at the church building or a home and bake a large batch of cookies. Have the teens do all the cooking, packaging and cleaning. When the cookies are ready take them to area nursing homes, or to the nurse stations at the hospitals. Try to arrange with the hospital to come at a shift change so the nurses leaving can take some cookies home, and those who are coming on can start their shift on a positive note.

3 Clean houses. Teens do not have the reputation for keeping their rooms neat. Blow your congregation away by offering their house cleaning services. Designate a Saturday and ask your church members to sign up a week in advance to have their house cleaned. Provide the service free of charge, but humbly accept any donations to add to the youth fund.

4 **Repair a home.** Here is a big project that will require more than just you and the teens. Ask for some contractors in your congregation to lend a hand. There is probably someone in your church that needs some repair work done to their home. If not, call the city and ask about anyone who has called asking for assistance in this area. If that fails, call Habitat for Humanity to learn about getting involved in their program.

5 **Rake and run**. Load your teens up in the fall armed with rakes and trash bags. Go to church members homes who have lots of trees and rake their yards. Don't tell them you're coming, just show up and get to work. Make a contest of it each year and see how many yards you can do in a day.

6 **Free car wash.** The morning of your car wash have teens go door to door in your churches' neighborhood handing out free car wash tickets. When the people come have the teens wash and rinse without fee or donation. Say, "Our only charge is that you would be our guest at our worship services at some point." Hand them a card from the church stating service times and tell them to have a great day.

> "The Son of Man did not come to be served, but to serve."
> - Mark 10:45

7 **Volunteer workday.** Schools and civic organization are always in need of volunteers. Contact the area schools and find out what day they work on their grounds. Show up and help them pick up trash, weed flowerbeds, etc.

Another way to help your community is by volunteering

to serve in a soup kitchen. If your town furnishes meals for the needy in your community, call and designate a day when your group would be available to serve.

8 **Senior Saints fruit baskets.** The seniors of your congregation have paved the way for others to enjoy freedom in Christ. Honor them by having the teens make fruit baskets and homemade cards, and delivering them to the homes of your seniors. Tell them personally how much you appreciate everything they have done through the years to make your church what it is.

9 **Canned food drive.** During the months of September and October, place a large box in your youth room to collect canned goods. Challenge the teens to bring them every Sunday morning during those months so you will be able to help needy families have a good Thanksgiving and Christmas. To make it more personal, adopt a specific family to help. Take their picture and place it on the box so teens will know their work will help someone they know. When the time comes to deliver the food, ask for several teens to help. They will get to meet the family, or families, that received the blessing of your group.

10 **Rummage sale.** Yard and garage sales are more popular than ever. If people think they will get a deal, they'll get up at 3 a.m. and park in front of a house until the sale begins (I'm not kidding).

Use your church parking lot to have a huge sale. Ask members a month in advance to donate worthy items, and to bring them the day of the sale to the church. To help in the cause, select a charity that all proceeds will be donated to. People will respond to need.

When adults were polled about what made the greatest impact on their lives during their teens years in church, the top two responses were mission trips and service projects.

SEVENTEEN

10 Tips for a Life of Joy

1 **Be thankful.** "Give thanks in all circumstances, for this is God's will for you in Christ Jesus," I Thessalonians 5:18. Live with a thankful spirit. Get out a sheet of paper, or use the left margin, and list ten things you are thankful for at this moment. When you complete the list, pray and thank God specifically for each item.

The challenge made by the Holy Spirit in this verse is that our circumstances should not dictate our thankfulness. Since all things work together for good for those who love the Lord (Romans 8:28), blessings and curses ought to cause thanksgiving.

2 **Lose sight of self.** "Do nothing out of selfish ambition or ill conceit, but in humility consider others better than yourself. Each of you should look not only on your own interests, but also the interests of others," Philippians 2:3-4. If you are like me, you would rather have your way than not have it. Satan envelops our hearts with selfishness and if we don't get what we want we get bitter, which is the opposite of joy.

To keep a spirit of joy surrounding you, find ways to make another person's day. Leave encouraging notes around the office. Volunteer your time to help people who are not as blessed. When we lose sight of self and place it on others, we place our eyes on God at the same time.

3 **Give.** "Just as you excel in everything - in faith, in speech, in knowledge, in complete earnestness and in your love for us - see that you also excel in this grace of giving," II Corinthians 8:7. Giving may mean time or money or both.

Jesus made it clear; there is more blessing, more joy, in giving than receiving (Acts 20:35).

4 **Sing.** "Is anyone of you in trouble? He should pray. Is anyone happy? Let him sing songs of praise," James 5:13. It's tough to sing when you are sad, but when there's joy, let it rip. Sing songs of praise to the Lord for His goodness and greatness. Don't save your songs for the "worship" hour. Sing in the shower. Sing as you drive to work. Sing during your breaks. Not only is it hard to sing when your sad, it's hard to get sad when you sing.

5 **Rest.** "Come to me, all you who are weary and burdened and I will give you rest," Matthew 11:28. In our workaholic society rest has become a dirty four letter word. In ministry you have those who accuse you of not working at all. Knocking yourself out with activities and events to prove your worth and your salary can end up making you worthless. It is impossible to be productive when you're exhausted.

Even Jesus knew He needed time away from the crowds. I figured out a long time ago that I'm not Jesus, and if He needed rest to keep His life focused and joy-filled, then so do I - and so do you.

6 **Walk with God.** "Enoch walked with God," Genesis 5:24. That's a peaceful phrase isn't it? It's a phrase of intimacy, and phrase of relationship. Develop a personal relationship with God and know joy. No relationship is more complete or secure.

7 **Form friendships.** "Wounds from a friend can be trusted," Proverbs 27:6a. Ministry can be a lonely existence. You have a church full of acquaintances, but that does not guarantee a friend. How many friends do you have right now? Have you been too busy for friendship to keep you accountable, and to get your mind

off the flock for a while? If so, get busy developing the needed friendship of others, then write your present friend(s) a note thanking them for their friendship.

8 **Obey God.** "If you obey my commands, you will remain in my love...I have told you this so that my joy may be in you and that your joy may be complete," John 14:10-11. Obedience brings blessings and disobedience delivers consequences. Which from God's hand would you rather have? God said long ago that His commands were designed for our good, not our detriment (Deuteronomy 10:12-13). Knowing and doing the will of God, as Jesus says, makes your joy complete.

9 **Avoid extremes.** "...the man who fears God will avoid extremes," Ecclesiates 7:18. A "sky is falling" mentality will rob you of all joy. If everything is a crisis in your book then thank God for the ulcer you are about to develop. Ministry is not the place for a completely carefree attitude, but it is the place to be care free (I Peter 5:7).

10 **Smile and laugh - a lot.** "Rejoice in the Lord always. I will say it again: Rejoice!" Philippians 4:4. Some writers say that Paul had to say it twice or Christians wouldn't have believed it would be okay.

Have a light heart and take joy with you everywhere you go by enjoying each moment God has given you. There are enough Christians out there who look sour, so there's no need for you to join that bunch.

EIGHTEEN

10 Ways to Involve Parents

1 **Bible Class teachers.** One advantage to using parents to teach is that they have teens of their own, possibly in the class they are instructing. They know the needs of teens and some of the issues they are facing.

Because of the up front nature of this role, try to acquire a parent with teaching skills. You don't want to kill your class with boredom just to get a parent involved.

2 **Event planners.** Combine parents and teens and let them plan out the year's activities together. Parents will be aware of upcoming events and will be more supportive since they helped plan them.

Get parents involved in the dream and vision process by asking them to list the reasons for a particular event. If your group is planning a mission trip, give your parents a "dream sheet" to write down everything they hope will be accomplished through the trip. This not only involves them, but allows them to see trips as a tool for ministry.

3 **Chaperones.** No matter how much teens beg to go it alone, chaperones are needed. Assign parents a group of four or five teens to minister to on a trip. Provide a specific list of responsibilities for the parents to follow so they will know what is expected; things such as making sure the teens in your group stay together or getting them back to the van five minutes ahead of departure time.

4 **Small group leaders.** If you host a small group you obviously can't be at and lead each one. Most parents would love to help facilitate a group, and most have leadership skills that they never get to use in the church.

If you are unsure about the abilities of some of your parents, have them go through a small group leadership training class. Base it on the training given to your adult small group leaders. All that may be required is a little tweaking to make it conducive for teen groups.

5 **Prayer parents.** The tools mentioned so far call for parents' involvement in a visible way. This calls for their invisible involvement.

Divide your parents into twelve groups and assign each group a month. On the first Sunday of each month print out the names of all the teens in your group and give a copy to the parents assigned for that particular month. As a praying parent, have them pray over each name specifically daily for the entire month.

6 **Retreat and camp counselors.** Most camps and retreats hire people who are only a few years older than the teens present to be their counselors. If you have some parents who would be great at camp, call ahead of time and get permission to bring them along as assistant counselors.

7 **Devotionals and social activities hosts.** There are a ton of parents out there who feel they could never lead a devotional, or singing, but who are more than willing to open their home to the group. Make a sign up sheet available for parents who are willing to use their homes for special events. The change of atmosphere will be encouraging to the teens, and the parents will feel that they are getting to serve the group in a special way.

8 **Van and bus drivers.** With trips over two hours in length, recruit parents to help drive. Believe it or not, most teens don't mind if their parents drive. It gives them the perfect opportunity to critique their lack of skills on the asphalt!

Before assigning your parents to a road trip, be sure they have the proper license and are included on the vehicle insurance. Most states allow a personal driver's license for vehicles with fifteen or fewer passengers. For vehicles with more than fifteen, you may be required to have a CDL (Commercial Driver's License). Check your state requirements.

9 **Parent Advisors.** Use these people as research and development in your ministry.

- Have them surf the net for ministry ideas, keeping a list of the web sites visited and what may be useful to your ministry.
- Have them attend youth ministry conferences with you. Usually there are too many classes being offered for you to attend all of them, so send parents to the ones you can't attend.
- Have them visit different churches in the areas to interview other youth ministers to discover what has been successful for them.

A Parent Advisory Committee will not only provide valuable information for your ministry, but will also give parents an inside view of youth ministry.

10 **Volunteer counselors.** Survey your parents to discover if there are any with counseling experience. If so, ask if they would mind sharing your counseling load. Both of you benefit from this arrangement. Parents get to use an ability to serve the kingdom, and you get the freedom to use your energy in another area.

NINETEEN

10 Tips for Setting S.M.A.R.T. G.O.A.L.S.

1 **Specific.** Begin setting goals by getting specific. Nail down your desire to enable a clear picture in exact terms. A general goal may be, "I want to read more this year." A specific goal would define "more" and the books on the "to read" list. Specific: "I will read one new book a month in this order..."

The more specific a goal, the greater the chance of it being reached. Think in general terms and receive general results. Think in specific terms and accomplish your imagination.

2 **Measurable.** In the book example above a measurement wouldn't be hard to keep up with. Each month you measure what you accomplished by what you wanted to accomplish. If you read a book, the goal for the month became reality. If only half a book was read, your measurement shows that only half the goal was met.

Other goals are not as easy to measure, nor as tangible. Perhaps your goal is to lessen the stress in your life by relying on others to take some of the responsibility. The only measurement you have that your stress is reduced is by feel. Or if you went at this goal from a very specific angle your blood pressure may be the measurement for this goal.

3 **Attainable**. At my stature and age "to be an NBA all-star by the time I'm thirty-five" isn't attainable. In place of that dream I may make a goal "to make twenty consecutive three pointers, so I can beat my partner at h.o.r.s.e." The goal is reachable, but not without effort. Stretch yourself by setting challenging goals that are attainable.

4 **Rewarding.** Will you yawn at the end of the goal? What is the carrot at the end of the stick? A new physique? A great vocabulary? Bragging rights? On the day of goal completion what type of celebration have you planned?

When I received my college degree (mom was proud I crammed a four year degree program into eleven years), my salary did not increase, but my self esteem did. The reward associated with my degree, besides knowledge, is accomplishment. What will your reward be?

5 **Timed.** Set a time limit for your goal or you may end up in school for eleven years. Like #1 and #3, it needs to be specific and attainable. Suppose I decide "to lose forty pounds in a month." That *might* be attainable, but it is definitely unhealthy. However, losing forty pounds in forty weeks can be reached in a healthy fashion. From that, I can mark out forty weeks on the calendar to meet the goal. One pound a week. Just 500 less calories a day. That's only a candy bar and a half!

> A goal without a plan is nothing more than a wish.

6 **Godly.** Is this goal something that will bring God glory? Will it help me do His will more effectively? Do I want this goal for selfish reasons? Measure your motives to make sure the goal you have in mind is fit for the kingdom. Do you have a goal to become a public speaker? Is that to honor God, or to honor yourself? Ask God to search your heart and reveal only goals that will help you remain humble and purposed for His work.

7 **Outlined.** Get a sheet of paper and write goal number one on the top line. List these terms down the left side leaving plenty of room to write between them: Specific, Measurable, Attainable, Rewarding, Timed, and Godly.

Outline each goal you have by defining it in those terms. Write it as specific as possible. Be sure it is attainable though challenging. Record the reward of its accomplishment. Write down a specific date the goal will be completed. Pencil in the ways this goal will propel you toward God's will.

8 **Accountable.** Don't goal it alone. Select a friend to call you at least once a week to ask about the goal you are working toward. Be honest and confess how you fell apart, or how it is easier than you thought it would be. Give your goal accountability partner permission to be sneaky and check up on you when you don't expect it.

9 **Life changing.** Select goals that will change you over the long haul of life. The secret of life-changing goals comes through a changed lifestyle, such as changed eating habits, or through a learned experience, such as reading twelve books in a year, or climbing a mountain. As your life drifts from the date the goal became reality continue to draw from the experience. Let your goal setting have a lasting impact on your way of living.

10 **Self-disciplined.** Once you make the decision to work toward a goal, stick with it until you accomplish it. Get mentally tough and don't let up until the goal is met.

TWENTY

10 Tools for Teen Faith Development

1 **God's power.** Jesus said, "No one can come to me unless the Father draws Him" (John 6:44). This is the number one tool for a teen's faith development. God draws a teen into a relationship with Him. God convicts the heart and creates the need for salvation. God grants grace and forgiveness. God's power makes all this possible.

Relying on God's power will forge true faith in a teen. Relying on our power may result in the teen's faith being in us. Paul wrote that he came "to preach the gospel - not with words of human wisdom, less the cross be emptied of it's power" (I Corinthians 1:17). Our human wisdom only weakens the message. Let God bring power to your group.

2 **Daily Bible Study.** "Faith comes by hearing, and hearing by the word of God" (Romans 10:17). The Bible contains the actual words of God. A teen's faith matures when he or she believes that statement and lives it.

Before turning to their friends, teach your group to turn to God first. Our sinfulness allows us to rationalize almost any wrong into a right. God's Word, however, remains true. The more an individual reads and lives the Word, the stronger their faith gets, and the more dependent on God they become. (Teen Life Slide Rules are a great tools for getting teens into the Word.)

3 **A faith that works.** Provide opportunities for your teens to put their faith into action. James, Jesus' brother, recorded it this way, "Show me your faith without deeds, and I will show you my faith by what I do" (James 2:18).

There exists a direct correlation between faith and works. When we have faith we work. When we work for the Lord, faith develops. You've seen it before. A teen with great faith believes God will do great things, so she saves all the money she can for the mission trip. Another teen holds weak faith and goes on the trip for fun. But as he sees God changing lives through his group, his life changes and his faith grows.

4 **Testimonies.** In a similar way, teens can grow through the testimony of other believers. Your church contains people whom your teens look up to and respect. They know nothing of their past but only know the good of their present. Contact a couple of members who you know have a "checkered," but forgiven, past. Invite them to class to tell their stories of how Christ transformed their lives.

5 **Discipleship.** "Go and make disciples..." Jesus commanded. Whether you use the term discipleship or mentoring, the key is to get a mature believer into the life of a teen with immature faith. This person continually points the teen toward Jesus.

Don't assign a disciple to a teen without first thinking it through carefully. Remember the phrase, "Christians are born, disciples are made." Making a teen a devoted follower of Christ will take more than an occasional pat on the back and a quick prayer. Choose a discipler who will invest in the life of a teen by being available, offering an open heart, and displaying a blameless example.

6 **Prayer journals.** "If you believe, you will receive whatever you ask for in prayer" (Matthew 21:22). Encourage your teens to keep a prayer journal to further develop their faith. When times are tough it's hard to see God, but a prayer journal will be proof of God's presence in their lives.

Teens can use a common notebook for journaling. Tell them to write down their prayer requests each time they pray along with the date. Have them leave space to fill in the ways God answered the prayer.

7 **Workbooks.** "I meditate on your precepts and consider your ways" (Psalm 119:15). *Experiencing God* and other workbooks have become popular with good reason. These tools take a believer on a journey through a subject on a deep level. It helps the individual see God's hand in their day to day lives. A workbook can offer guidance on a subject while allowing personal discovery. Teens who are committed enough to set aside thirty minutes a day devoted to God's Word and a workbook study guide will be on the fast track of faith maturity.

8 **Books and music.** "For where your treasure is, there your heart will be also" (Matthew 6:21). Give your group members as many positive influences as possible to aid their faith. Provide a list of top selling Christian books for them to read. Play Christian artists at your meetings. Whether they want to admit it or not teens know that what they read and listen to effects their faith. One group I know of got so convicted about that after a youth convention that they destroyed all their secular CDs when they got home - over $2400 worth!

9 **Family Devotionals.** "These commandments I give you today are to be upon your hearts. Impress them on your children..." (Deuteronomy 6:6-7a). Dare I say it? A majority, though not all, of teens with weak faith have parents of weak faith. Or parents of strong faith who allow their teens to adopt their faith without owning it. God expects parents to be the chief faith developers of their children.

10 **Personal prayer.** Pray for every teen in your group everyday. Ask God to give them a faith that will move mountains.

Twenty One

10 Verses to Memorize

1 **John 3:16-17**.
16 For God so loved the world that he gave his one and
only Son, that whoever believes in him shall not perish
but have eternal life.
17 For God did not send his Son into the world to
condemn the world, but to save the world through him.

2 **Ephesians 2:8-10**.
8 For it is by grace you have been saved, through faith-
-and this not from yourselves, it is the gift of God-- 9 not
by works, so that no one can boast.
10 For we are God's workmanship, created in Christ
Jesus to do good works, which God prepared in advance
for us to do.

3 **Psalm 23**.
1 The LORD is my shepherd, I shall not be in want.
2 He makes me lie down in green pastures, he leads me
beside quiet waters,
3 he restores my soul. He guides me in paths of
righteousness for his name's sake.
4 Even though I walk through the valley of the shadow
of death, I will fear no evil, for you are with me; your rod
and your staff, they comfort me.
5 You prepare a table before me in the presence of my
enemies. You anoint my head with oil; my cup overflows.
6 Surely goodness and love will follow me all the days of
my life, and I will dwell in the house of the LORD forever.

4. Deuteronomy 6:4-9.

4 Hear, O Israel: The LORD our God, the LORD is one.
5 Love the LORD your God with all your heart and with all your soul and with all your strength.
6 These commandments that I give you today are to be upon your hearts.
7 Impress them on your children. Talk about them when you sit at home and when you walk along the road, when you lie down and when you get up.
8 Tie them as symbols on your hands and bind them on your foreheads.
9 Write them on the doorframes of your houses and on your gates.

5. Matthew 28:19-20.

19 Therefore go and make disciples of all nations, baptizing them in the name of the Father and of the Son and of the Holy Spirit,
20 and teaching them to obey everything I have commanded you. And surely I am with you always, to the very end of the age.

6. Mark 12:30-31.

30 "'Love the Lord your God with all your heart and with all your soul and with all your mind and with all your strength.'
31 The second is this: 'Love your neighbor as yourself.' There is no commandment greater than these."

7. Philippians 4:13.

13 I can do everything through him who gives me strength.

8. I Corinthians 15:1-4.

1 Now, brothers, I want to remind you of the gospel I preached to you, which you received and on which you have taken your stand.
2 By this gospel you are saved, if you hold firmly to the word I preached to you. Otherwise, you have believed in vain.
3 For what I received I passed on to you as of first importance : that Christ died for our sins according to

the Scriptures,
4 that he was buried, that he was raised on the third day according to the Scriptures.

9. **Psalm 100.**

1 Shout for joy to the LORD, all the earth.
2 Worship the LORD with gladness; come before him with joyful songs.
3 Know that the LORD is God. It is he who made us, and we are his ; we are his people, the sheep of his pasture.
4 Enter his gates with thanksgiving and his courts with praise; give thanks to him and praise his name.
5 For the LORD is good and his love endures forever; his faithfulness continues through all generations.

10 **Revelation 22:17,20.**

17 The Spirit and the bride say, Come! And let him who hears say, Come! Whoever is thirsty, let him come; and whoever wishes, let him take the free gift of the water of life.
20 He who testifies to these things says, Yes, I am coming soon. Amen. Come, Lord Jesus.

Psalm 119:11 I have hidden your word in my heart that I might not sin against you.

Use this space to write down your favorite verses in the Bible.

TWENTY TWO

10 Traits of a Strong Youth Group

1 **Christ Centered.** A lot of problems handle themselves when a group is totally centered around Jesus. Within your group there may be personality and social problems, but a majority of these will be minor with Jesus in the middle.

Reasons a group may have tensions are numerous. Leading the list, however, is selfishness. As the leader, model the unselfish attitude of Christ. Keep the cross before your teens at all times and have that as the goal. When your teens get self-centered instead of Christ-centered, stop and have the group pray on the spot. Too often our groups have problems and we accept it as part of the job. Turn it over to God. They may not mind fighting each other. They will mind fighting Him.

2 **Prayer Oriented.** Is prayer the first inclination of your group before making decisions or when facing trials? A group that prays together, stays together for several reasons. First, prayer is the acknowledgement that your power is not great enough to make what you are asking happen. Second, teens with different cultural and social backgrounds can speak to Jesus together even if they don't speak to each other otherwise. Third, asking and receiving allow us to see God working. God works without prayer, but we fail to see it because we don't expect it. When we ask specifically for something and it happens, we recognize it and give God the glory. A youth group filled with prayer warriors will see God's

handy- work at every interval.

3 **Daily Worshippers.** Worship means that we bow, or kiss, one greater than ourselves. How often do our groups bow before the Lord? Many who were raised in the church see Sunday as "the day" of worship. But doesn't the Lord deserve daily praise?

Fill your group with daily worshippers and you will discover a group that has a greater love for one another, and a greater love for God. Why? Because bowing immediately lowers our personal wants and we then realize that we are in the presence of one greater than ourselves. If your group does not practice kneeling and bowing as you worship together, give it a try. Our hearts and our physical responses are linked. Bow in your group and see if your teens don't enter a new spirit of worship.

4 **Parent-Involved.** Family ministry receives a lot of press today. Parents can make positive contributions to a ministry because of their love for their children, and because of their desire to see their teens saved.

Another term for parental support is trust. When the parents trust you, the risk you take to get teens to the next spiritual level, or to get more teens saved, will be appreciated and supported. You've heard the expression, "Trust must be earned." Earn their trust by involving parents in youth ministry and developing the first three items on this list in the lives of their children.

5 **Outreach Oriented.** Have you ever noticed youth shepherds who keep their sheep corralled safely away from other sheep? Their goal, it seems, is to keep the sheep they have. They are not excited about the prospect of gaining more sheep, and definitely not wanting a sheep to leave their pen for another.

Jesus said a shepherd should be willing to leave the ninety-nine and go after the one who was lost. Create a lost sheep mentality in your group that is not willing for any to perish (II Peter 3:9).

6 **Mission Minded.** Not only do great groups look for the lost around them, they are willing to "go into all the world

and make disciples."

7 United. Unity without "i" is un-ty. Keeping a group united requires every member being tied into the body of Christ. Paul wrote in I Corinthians 1:10, "I appeal to you, brothers, in the name of our Lord Jesus Christ, that you all agree with one another so that there may be no divisions among you and that you may be perfectly united in mind and thought."

8 Serving. Planning service projects does not mean you have servants in your group. A true servant spirit serves out of love, not obligation. When a servant spirit exists in a group, excitement, not complaining, persists whether they are cleaning homes, raking yards, washing cars, or picking up trash on the side of the road. A servant group has learned from experience that whoever wants to be great must be "the servant of all" (Mark 9:35).

9 Taking care of each other. Have you heard the one about the youth group that couldn't get along? It's not a joke, there really are groups like that. Some kids get teased for their speech impediment while others get made fun of for maturing late, or not looking good. Great groups, however, take care of and protect each member. Each individual sees every other teen in the group as part of the body of Christ. They know that when they make fun of another teen, they make fun of Jesus.

10 Maturing. No group has "arrived" and strong youth groups know it. They understand that their group uses "works of service, so that the body of Christ might be built up until [all teens] reach unity in the faith and in the knowledge of the Son of God and become mature, attaining to the whole measure of the fullness of Christ" (Ephesians 4:12-13). Strong groups also grow by "forgetting what is behind and straining toward what is ahead" (Philippians 3:13).

TWENTY THREE

10 Techniques to Reach Unchurched Teens

1 **Love them with your whole heart.** It's hard to believe the number of children in the world who never hear, "I love you." By the time those kids get to be teens their hearts are callused and closed to those who would love them. They may hear you say "I love you," but they probably won't believe it. Listen to the counsel of John, "Dear children, let us not love with words or in tongue but with actions and in truth" (I John 3:18). To reach unchurched teens, don't just tell them you love them, *show* them.

2 **Be genuine and honest.** For years the Coca-Cola Company used the slogan, "It's the real thing." Well, teens want to see the "real thing" in you. With all the virtual reality that surrounds their lives, it's refreshing when they find someone who is exactly what they say and seem.

Reach unchurched teens by letting your "yes" be "yes" and your "no" be "no." Be true to your word. If you say that you will pick a teen up after school for a quick pick-up game of basketball, be at the meeting spot on time. Just like adults, teens are used to people making empty promises. Make sure your promises and life are the real thing.

3 **Be friendly and accepting.** Here's the scenario. Your top evangelistic teen reached out to the tattoo king of the school and invited him to your Sunday morning class. Of course, having never attended church, this fascinating fellow owns no suitable attire. As he glides into your room, you're caught off guard by the splashing mermaid located on the right bicep of his sleeveless shirt. You're mesmerized. You don't want to stare, but you have to. He stares back. "Nice tatt..to meet you," you muster.

That is not a paragraph of being friendly and accepting. Regardless of how a teen dresses, or how their body may be carved, extend an enthusiastic hand and a warm authentic welcome. Who knows, if you keep that up this guy might bring his whole gang of splashing mermaids to the Lord.

4 **Create a first class ministry.** Do everything in your ministry to the best of your ability. It's better to do two things well, than ten things poorly. Whether you think it is fair or not, visitors do decide whether or not to return based on what they see. If an unchurched teen enters and can tell that teens and your ministry are an important part of your church, you've gone a long way in getting him/her to return.

5 **Big events.** Make it a goal to plan at least one major event a year to reach the teens in your area. Do whatever it takes to get a crowd, a really big crowd. Battle of the Bands? Water Wars? Name it what you want, and do what you want with no cost to guests. The only thing you require of those who come is for them to fill out an address card.

6 **Promotion.** Plaster posters all over the city. Have Christian clubs announce your activities at school. Supply your teens with invitation cards that tell the when, where, and why of your group. Do a mail-out to the list you gathered in #5. Use logos and slogans that relate to teen culture.

There are so many angles in promoting an activity that it may not be possible to use them all, just don't overlook word-of-mouth as being the greatest source of promotion.

Keep your teens informed of every activity, but especially activities which will be conducive for inviting their lost friends.

7 **Meet needs.** "Kids ought to come to Christ because He is Lord and not to get their needs met!" Nobody ever came to the Lord without wanting a need met. On the day of Pentecost the crowd cried, "What must we do to be saved?" What did they need? Salvation. What did they get? Salvation. Take a survey of your church to see if anyone there didn't come to Christ out of a need.

Jesus often met the needs of the people physically before He touched their lives spiritually. If an unchurched teen comes to your group looking for a friend, be one to him. Allow needs to be the gateway to a changed life.

8 **Provide other people for the unchurched to connect with.** You may be ultra-cool, but you still can't reach every teen. Upon meeting a teen in need of Christ, try to think of another teen or adult who could befriend them. Call them ahead of time to tell them a little bit about their new disciple, then find a convenient time and place for them to meet.

9 **Network with teens in your group.** On the count of three, name all the classmates in your most popular teen's fourth period class. One. Two. Three...What do you mean you can't do it? What? Your teens know who is in their classes better than you do? Okay, then get your teens to tell you about their classmates. Ask every teen in your group to pick who they think are the top two prospects for Jesus in their classes. Get the list, get your group, and get on to #10.

10 **Get on their turf.** If the unchurched teens won't come to you, go to them. Ask your group to introduce you to all their friends. Have them point out the top prospects. Use football, basketball and all other activities at school as a way to talk to them abouut Jesus.

Special Tip: When you meet teens remember their names. If they decide to visit your church and you call them by name, they will never forget it.

TWENTY FOUR

10 Tips for Staying Mentally Healthy

1 **Stretch your faith.** "We walk by faith, not by sight" II Corinthians 5:7. Take the pressure off of yourself and place it on God, which is what He wants anyway. Our egos tell us to do all we can, then just before we fall apart, hand it over to the Lord. That's not faith, it's desperation. Trade in safe faith for stretched faith.

Walking by faith keeps ministers mentally healthy because they know the outcome is not dependant on them. They place their troubles on God and expect His purposes to be fulfilled.

2 **Remove all 'stinkin' thinkin'.** Protect your mind from negative influences by letting Philippians 4:8 be a filter for your heart, "Finally, brothers, whatever is true, whatever is noble, whatever is right, whatever is pure, whatever is lovely, whatever is admirable - if anything is excellent or praiseworthy - think about such things." Using that verse to permit or prohibit certain thoughts or materials from entering your brain will make a difference.

What does this translate into in practical terms? No dirty or off-color jokes, language that glorifies, reading materials with no questionable content - or photographs. Ministers are not excluded from temptation, so protect your mental and spiritual health by applying this tip.

3 **Read and listen to uplifting materials.** Who are your favorite motivational authors and speakers? Zig Ziglar?

John Maxwell? Allow God to minister to you through those He gifted to motivate His people.

What are your favorite magazines and books? *Leadership* and *Group* are fantastic magazines whose ministry is also an occupation. *Discipleship Journal* is awesome reading for any believer who wants to be transformed into the image of Jesus. If you take advantage of as many of these tools as possible, you'll be blessed.

4 **Share your problems.** I hope you have a person you can trust and talk with about your struggles. Keeping troubles corked on the inside of your life is a quick way to mental illness. If you have a friend you can trust for counsel, great. If not, and you know your burdens are affecting your life, see a professional counselor. This doesn't mean you have serious psychological problems. It only means you need someone you can trust to relieve the stress of ministry.

5 **Rise above mediocrity.** Anyone can be average. Anyone can do the minimum. Follow the example set by Jesus and "do all things well." Let your name be synonymous with excellence.

By striving for the best, you will feel better about yourself, and your teens will be the recipients of God's blessings through you.

6 **Be child-like.** "Daddy, Daddy! Look, look!" I almost lost control of the car on the interstate because of my child's yelling.

"What?! What is it?!" I respond frantically imagining a deer was about to lurch into our path.

"Up there!" Steven, our three year old, points.

I look but don't see anything. "What do you see?"

"The moon."

When is the last time you stood in awe of the moon and stars? When last did the oceans waves crash on your feet to your amazement? Return to childhood and let your senses soak up all the wonders of God's creation.

7 **Learn from failure.** Zig Ziglar says, "Failure is an event, not a person." When you fail, you have just succeeded in

learning one way not to do something. To learn from failing ask yourself four questions:

1. How would I do that differently if I could do it again?
2. What aspects did go right?
3. What adjustments need to be made?
4. Who do I need to bring to make this succeed?

8 **Maintain a positive attitude.** *Twixt optimist and pessimist, the difference is quite droll. The optimist sees the donut the pessimist sees the hole.* Find something good in every circumstance and individual. Refuse to be the dark cloud on a sunny day.

A negative attitude siphons energy from yourself and others. A positive attitude keeps you feeling sharp and makes others want to be around you.

9 **Stay focused.** In the *10 Tips for Time Management* you were encouraged to keep a day timer. Keeping up with

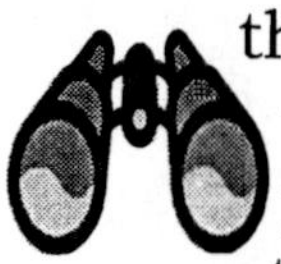

the details of the day will enable you to know your target and pursue it. Remaining focused will keep you from feeling drained by boredom. At the end of the day you will know exactly what you did and didn't accomplish.

An added advantage to being focused is the ability to provide a complete answer to a teen's or staff member's question, "What are you up to?" Out of habit most reply, "Nothing." Don't answer "nothing." Be focused and rattle off exactly what you've been up to.

10 **Be passionate.** What ignites your life? What gets your fire roaring? Even though people were making fun of him and threatening him with death, Jeremiah said, "Your word is like a fire shut up in my bones. I am weary of holding it in; indeed, I cannot." That's passion! Get some.

TWENTY FIVE

10 Tools for Affirming Teens

1 Jar of Affirmation. Place a jar in the middle of your classroom floor with a teen's name taped to it. Give each group member a piece of paper and a pencil to write an encouraging note to the person whose name is on the jar. The note might be about a mission experience, personal friendship, or just a note of appreciation. The only rule is that the note be positive. When all notes are completed, have the teens place them in the jar for the teen to take home and read. Next week have another jar with another teen's name on it. Do this each week until all teens have been encouraged.

2 A Penny for Your Thoughts. How many teens are in your group? ______ Multiply that number by three and bring that many pennies to class. (25 teens = 75 pennies.) Have your group sit in a circle, and tell them that you are about to toss some pennies into the middle of the circle. The goal if for them to collect as many as possible - no stealing pennies from others. When all the pennies are picked up, that indicates the number of positive comments they must make to other teen members. If a teen collects five pennies, they are required to encourage five people. If they have one, they encourage one. Place a jar in the middle of the room for teens to place their pennies into after each affirmation

they share.

3 **Poster Praise.** Get a sheet of poster board for each teen. At the top of each board write "I thank God for (teen's name) because..." Hang these boards up all over your room. During your class or devotional give each teen a marker and have them fill in the praise on each board. By the time they're done each teen should have written on everyone's poster board.

4 **Grab Bag.** Put the names of your youth group in a bag or box. Let each teen draw one name out of the box and write that person a letter of encouragement. This not only allows teens to affirm one another, but meet one another. Some teens will draw the name of someone they don't know very well. Their note may be general encouragement, but it will give them the chance to talk with someone they normally don't.

5 **Clothesline Kindness.** Hang a clothesline in your room with wooden clothespins attached. Write a teen's name on each clothespin until every teen has one. Provide small sheets of paper for teens to write notes to other teens in the group. Encourage them to write notes at home, or come early to class to do so, then use the clothespin to attach the mail. This gives new meaning to the term "pin" pal.

6 **Circle of Love.** Have your teens sit in a circle on the floor for this activity. Begin by working clockwise around the circle with each person completing this phrase "I love and appreciate you because..." to the person to their left.

Go around the circle again, only this time use a ball of twine. Let the first member hold the end and gently toss it to another group member. The person who tossed the ball gets to affirm the one who caught it. Reverse the process and have the catcher affirm the tosser. Do this until everyone has received encouragement and the ball returns to the one who began.

7 **Flashlight Nite.** Have teens form a circle or square. Turn out all the lights, and after

all the ooohs die out shine the flashlight on a teen (not in their eyes). Keep the teen illuminated for 30 seconds while the group affirms him or her. Repeat this for each teen until the entire group has been encouraged. Most teens love the spotlight so this ought to be a great night for them.

8 Picture Picture. Get a large corkboard and hang it in your office. Make a sign that says "World's #1 Youth Group" and place it above the board. Cover the board with pictures and encouraging notes the group has given you. When teens come hang out at your office, they'll notice that you really do care after all.

9 Play Favorites. Discover each teen's favorite dessert or junk food. Once a week go by the store with the names of a couple of teens and pick up their favorite morsels. Then go by their homes and make this special delivery.

10 C^2. Cards and calls may be old standbys, but they're hard to beat. Teens love to get mail - even from their youth leader. Make the card personal and encouraging. Point out a special gift God has given the teen and include the reason you thank God for him or her. If you are aware of a particular struggle mention in the letter that you are praying about it.

Use the telephone for general check-ups. In a letter teens don't have to respond verbally, on the phone they do. Don't be surprised if all you get is uh-huhs, but that doesn't mean they are not glad you called. It's the way they talk on the phone!

Don't let yourself go unaffirmed. When teens write you notes or letters telling you how great you are, don't throw them away. Place them in a drawer or a box and when those days come when you don't feel too special, take out those cards and reread them.

TWENTY SIX

10 Tips for Considering Leaving a Ministry

1 **When you lose vision and stop reaching goals.** Months may pass when little appears to be happening in your ministry, but you still have a dream, you still "press toward the prize in Jesus," as Paul puts it. When you no longer dream of a thriving ministry, when you stop pressing and start floating, it may be time to leave ministry.

2 **When you are not maturing spiritually.** Spiritual growth is a lifelong journey. Each year should take each member of the body of Christ closer to being like Him. While remaining the same may not signal the need to leave ministry, a serious fall without repentance may. Are you indifferent toward obedience? Do you sin and not care? Have the spiritual disciplines of your life fallen by the wayside?

3 **When you outgrow your ministry.** Some ministers are blessed enough for the church to help with their education and training while they are with that congregation. As a result of the gained degree, experience and education, you may be a blessing more somewhere else. God may place you with a small church to shape you for another role which will demand more and reward you more than your present ministry.

4 **When your ministry outgrows you.** Maybe you're not the mega-church type. You never planned for it to happen, but

your group, which started with ten, grew to 200 as a result of creative outreach. Most ministers would swell with pride, but you know God called you to minister to rural teens. The numbers are fine for others. In your heart you know this expanded ministry is too much to handle, and beyond your call.

5 **When your relationships with teens and their parents are severely strained.** As hard as it is to believe, you can't get along with everybody at some places. It may not be your fault. Maybe the last youth worker really was better than sliced bread. Or perhaps the last guy took advantage of a young girl in the group and parents vowed to never give their trust away again. Or maybe too many of the teens have been hurt and you don't see any hope until you graduate three groups. Whether you are or are not at fault, think about looking for a new position with this type of strain.

6 **When your philosophy is not the same as the leadership's or the congregation's.** Most fellowships require that you believe what they believe while you work for them and God (usually they think you are just working for them). Through study and friendships with other believers, you may discover you do not agree with everything your leader's do. Some issues may be minor, or you may discover major doctrinal differences. The former may not be reason to pack up, the later is good reason. First, because you are not being true to God. Second, the leadership will not want you teaching something they don't believe.

7 **When you have been emotionally or spiritually hurt.** Who in ministry doesn't have their battle scars? Parents gossiping about the way you treat their child. Teens daring you to cross the line. Elderships not trusting you to do your job. Of course those are light examples. A lot of people have been hurt severely in ministry. A close family member of mine is out of ministry because of the "brethren." If you find that you receive more abuse than support, don't leave the body, just leave that congregation.

8 **When attendance nose dives.** There are thousands of reasons for a decline in numbers. It could be that a major employer in the area shut down and families moved. If so, then stay. It could be that a new church started down the road that offers teens something more exciting. If so, then

stay. It may be that your church is dying because of ungodly decisions on the part of the leaders. If so, try to work them out and heal the church. If no relief is in sight, you know what to do. Or maybe, just maybe, it's you because of any of the tips previously mentioned.

9 When staff relationships are extremely strained. Is it possible that all ministers in the same office do not get along? Could the senior minister really be jealous? Why? Because you get the attention of the parents or because you get to go to amusement parks, retreats at the beach, and host a community Christmas party the size of Texas? Because when he goes out of town you fill in to preach and he hears, "You better get on it. That boy's good," when he returns? Because your personalities clash? Because your wives don't get along? Because he's the one that really shouldn't be in ministry, but you're the one having to move?

> Don't use this list to run. Instead, use it to evaluate where you feel you are presently. Never make a quick emotional decision when it comes to leaving a

10 When you have been offered an incredible salary somewhere else. In our book (and you're reading it) this is definitely a sign to get out the suitcases. When asked during an interview if he was in ministry "for the money," my co-author replied, "No. But my family's in it for every penny they can get." Seriously, in one regard ministry is, well, ministry. In another, it is an occupation that allows you to pay bills, and feed the people in your household. Salary is a tough issue because it seems so ungodly to want more money. But maybe it's God who's making the bigger pay check possible.

TWENTY SEVEN

10 TIPS FOR WASTING TIME

Do the opposite of these 10 tips, and you'll use God's time well.

1 **Spend a lot of time trying to decide what to do.** Assume the classic "thinker's pose" and sit for as long as you can. Don't use the night before to arrange your day. Don't structure the day first thing at the office.

2 **Watch Sports Center or classic movies.** Basically, do anything you can that is not ministry related. Pop a bag of corn and lean back in your chair and watch the day go by. Be sure to place a "do not disturb sign" on your door so there will be no interruptions that might cause you to have to do your job.

3 **Hang out with close friends, not with those who need Jesus.** Life goes by so fast. Why not spend all your time with friends? Ping-pong and pool are excellent ways to stay close to your buddies. Why not invite them to your office for the second tip in the list? Catch up on past memories and favorite stories (not related to ministry, of course).

4 **Take two hours for lunch and rest for a while when you return.** Mom always told you to chew your food well, right? It takes at least two hours to do that. What was her next piece of advice? Yep, lay down and let it digest. If possible see if you can get a couch placed in your office. Leather is nice and

comfortable. (Just in case some in the office don't believe a leather couch is a necessity, get into the "thinker's pose" when others walk by. This will prove you had to have it).

5 **Don't schedule appointments, let people stop by whenever they want.** Make an appointment only if someone insists, otherwise you'll have limited interruptions. By keeping an open door policy all day (except after lunch when your food is digesting), people can wander in and disturb you regularly. You can listen to the conversations going on outside your office. You can stroll out any time you want because no one will hear your door opening. And because you don't schedule appointments, no one can expect you to be there when they come by.

6 **Lay in bed an extra thirty minutes.** Practice slapping the snooze button six times. Here is a statement worth memorizing: If you start getting to work on time or - gasp - early, the staff will expect you to do it all the time. They'll start saying things like, "Why are you late?" followed with a suspicious stare. If you are late all the time they will never do that. Plus you will have succeeded in letting part of the day go by unproductively, which is the goal of this chapter.

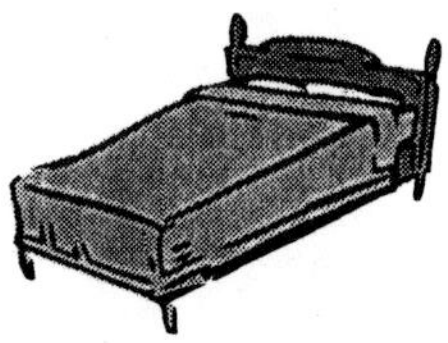

7 **Channel surf till all hours of the night.** Okay, we'll give you a reason to sleep in each morning. Watch all the late shows - at one time if possible. When those are over flip back and forth between "B" movies. Have you seen "The Crab Creature from Outer Space"? or, "Amazon Women of the Niagara"? If not, you haven't been channel surfing enough.

To help prepare you for these all-night sessions, buy one of those rubber stress balls to squeeze. Those rascals will strengthen your hands and fingers so you can use your remote control like a rocket for hours without tiring

8 **Hang around the water cooler and talk with the staff.** What? Your office doesn't have a water cooler? Then you have two options.

Option One: Spend a week researching water cooler companies on the web. Second, form a water cooler committee and set up meetings two nights a week for six weeks to go over your findings. Third, buy the cooler, but don't have it delivered. That might save time. Instead, go pick up the cooler yourself, preferably you bought one out of state. When you return set up the water cooler in a high traffic area and hang out by it.

Option two: Don't buy a water cooler. Call around to local businesses and ask if they have one. If they do, go over and hang out by theirs. This will get you out of the office, and help you avoid any ministry conversations.

9 **Stay on the phone talking with friends.** I have discovered that a wireless headset is best for this tip. Keep your favorite friends phone numbers on you at all time. When you finish a conversation with one, pull out the list and type the next number into the key pad attached to your belt or purse.

10 **Surf the net.** I mentioned the world wide web earlier for its usefulness in researching water coolers. Believe it or not there is a lot more info on the net beside water cooler information. It's true! Surf all you want during office hours, but deduct points for accidentally running across a web site that is religious in nature.

There you have it. Ten Tips for Wasting Time. Try these and we think you'll have more time to waste than you know what to do with. Before long you'll even have more time to waste because you and your water cooler will have to find other employment.

Though these tips were for fun, do be conscious of any time that you do waste and Make each moment productive for God.

TWENTY EIGHT

10 Do's for Counseling Teens

1 **Be available.** When teens are in need and you are "too busy" it makes a teen feel unimportant. If you don't have time for them, they will find someone, or something else that will. Allow teens with problems to approach you at any time. If time is pressing and you are busy at that moment, set a specific time for the two of you to get together. Explain why *now* is not the best time and assure the teen you will be available at the time you agreed on.

2 **Let teens know you love them.** In a counseling session it's important that a teen know you accept and love him or her. You may state this verbally or with your expressed concern.

Be cautious expressing your love for a teen of the opposite sex. People in counseling often look for love and may take your words farther than you intend. Express a Christ-like love that can't be mistaken for a physical love.

3 **Make teens feel comfortable.** Meet in non-threatening surroundings so a teen won't withdraw. Choose a location like a park, or fast food restaurant. Meet in an open place with plenty of people around. Your office is fine as long as the blinds on your door are open and other people are in the building. This protects you from possible rumors and temptation.

Use the first part of the session for small talk to relax the young person and to get it off on an interesting note.

Comfort is critical because the teen may feel insecure about seeing you for counseling, or her parents may have forced the issue.

4 **Keep all conversation confidential.** Have you ever had someone break a trust with you? Did you trust him again? Did you tell others about not trusting him?

Let all who come to you for counseling know that you will not share any of the conversation unless you suspect sudcide or breaking the law in any way. Don't share information with your spouse. Do not attempt to disguise the information as a devotional illustration.

The consequences for breaking a teen's trust are varied, but severe. They will probably tell everyone in the group not to trust you. If staff members discover that you don't keep counseling confidential they won't share information with you that is sensitive.

5 **Be a good listener.** Great counseling can take place with few words on your part. Listen. Listen. Listen. Even if the story is boring. Even if the problem isn't as tragic as the teen thinks. Smile, frown, cry with the one who came for your ear. Let each person know that you are listening will all of your heart.

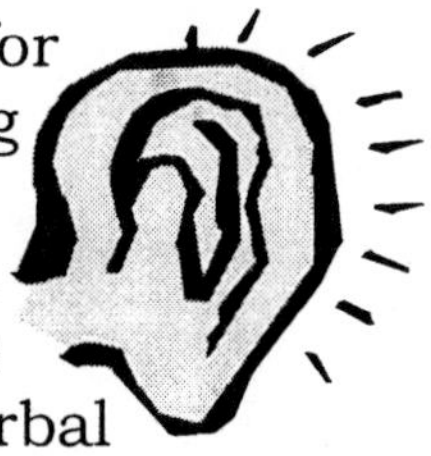

Use the techniques on page 51 to show that you are listening by repeating or interpreting what was said. Maintain eye contact and other non-verbal language to let the teen know you are paying attention.

6 **Pray during the sessions.** Begin and end your time together with prayer. This shows that you are handing things over to God and not depending on your own wisdom. It also gives the teen an opportunity to pour their heart out to God with an adult. Most teens have a prayer partner of their own age, but not someone older. Usually the older person is doing all the praying, so use this as a chance for the teen to form a prayer relationship with you.

7 **Help teens answer their own problems.** It's healthy and preferred if teens can come to their own solutions. If an adult constantly makes decisions for them, how will they learn to make them for themselves?

When the teen has shared the situation ask, "What are two things you can do to solve this dilemma?" Asking a teen to provide a number, in this case 2, of responses allows them to think critically. It provides options to choose from. "Well, I could... Or I could..."

8 **Teach when necessary.** We just suggested you help the teen make their own decisions, but there may be a time when you have to help them if they can't come to the right solution on their own. A guy thinking about suicide may not be able to think of one good reason for living. Teach him. A girl may not be able to see one thing wrong with abortion and will not come come to a godly solution, give her some godly options.

Resist the urge to teach them the solution unless you know the teen will not, or cannot, come to a satisfactory solution on their own.

9 **Find the root of the problem.** "I cheated on the test because I'm stupid and can't learn anything." That may be the top soil, but the root may lie in overbearing parents who demand too much. "I have sex because it's fun." That might hold some truth, but the root may be the girl feels ugly and she only feels loved during intercourse.

Whether they don't see it, or refuse to, most teens confess on the surface. We have taught believers to confess in general terms. "I have sinned," has become a blanket that allows us to keep from facing the root of the problem. Encourage those you counsel to be completely open and honest. Ask them to share what they feel the source of the problem is, not just the side issues.

10 **Attack the problem, not the person.** Said another way, "Hate the sin, love the sinner." When a teen comes to confess a specific sin let him or her know they made a mistake, not that they are a mistake.

Love each teen unconditionally as God has loved you unconditionally. Love each teen with compassion, but don't tolerate the sin.

TWENTY NINE

10 Tips for Planning Youth Activities

1 **Have a purpose in mind.** What do you want to accomplish with an event? Discipleship? Fellowship? Refreshment? Everything you plan should have a reason behind it. Why? Because events for events sake breeds superficialness. It communicates that ministry exists to look good. By stating a specific purpose for each activity teens will learn the "whys" behind every activity.

For example, your group decides to make giant Christmas cards out of poster board for members of your church who can't attend because of physical problems. Teens might think you're doing it simply because it's nice. That's a good reason but a better one is that Jesus said, "If you give a cup of cold water to the least of my brothers, you have done it to me." Let the group know that by serving shut-in members, they are serving Jesus. Find a scriptural basis for every event and give meaning to the method.

2 **Don't be afraid to be creative.** You don't have to do things differently all the time, but don't be afraid to get crazy some of the time. "What if I look like an idiot?" Great! Who cares if we look dumb in the process of sharing Jesus?

Look at things from a different angle. Jesus did. Who else would describe the Pharisees as whitewashed tombs? What about the time He told Peter how to fish? Remember, He was a carpenter!

As you plan events ask question like, "How can we make this better?" "How can we make this unforgettable?" "How can we make this exciting?"

3 **Go first class.** Going first-class may mean you have five events instead of ten. Never throw something together just so there will be more on the calendar. Put as much time and effort as you can into every event. That will prevent parents from saying, "This sure seems unorganized. Are you sure you thought about this before having it?" It will also prevent your teens from saying to the friend they invited, "I'm sorry. Usually our stuff is better than this."

4 **Use plenty of chaperones for each event.** Not only will this involve parents and other members of the church, it will keep you from having to keep one eye on Susy and Johnny and their tendency to slip into the shadows for a quick smooch.

Shoot for one chaperone for every ten teens. The place won't seem loaded with adults and you won't feel overburdened by the crowd. Be sure to let chaperones know their exact responsibility, which should be somewhere between Gomer Pyle and Sergeant Carter.

5 **Make a list and check it twice.** Write down *everything* you will need. Don't rely on mental notes to get you prepared and through an event. Get a sheet of paper and a pen, and write legibly in case you divide the list with someone else. As you complete an item mark it off the list. You may want to put your "to do's" in order from beginning to end, or from first to least importance.

6 **Promote! Promote! Promote!** The best activity is worthless if you don't tell anyone about it. It's great to have a great activity, but you know what? It's even greater to have a great activity if the teens show up! Use flyers, phone, email, website, radio, newsletters, word of mouth, school announcement centers, whatever it takes to get the word out. If people don't show because they didn't want to come, that's one thing. It's another if they don't show because they didn't know.

7 **Be excited.** Approach an event like it's a "ho-hum" activity and the teens will do the same. Enthusiasm is contagious so share it freely with your group.

Perhaps you haven't noticed, but this book contains lists of tens. Make your own ten list for each event. "Ten Reason to Come to "The Greatest Show on Earth." "Top Ten Ways to Have an Awesome Time at Camp Sumatonga! Some are even Legal." "Ten Survival Tips for Friday's Lock-in." Let your passion for an event shine through.

8 **Plan spiritual times carefully.** Every event may not be conducive for a full blown devotional, but even visitors will think something's up if there is no prayer for the refreshments. As you plan, think about which moment might be best to talk about the Lord. Which would work better? Mentioning up front that you believe the Lord brought everyone for a purpose would work? Or closing with "We hope you felt the love of the Lord tonight. No offense to those who LOST! at broom hockey"? However you decide to talk about the Lord, just be sure you don't throw it in because it's a youth event and that's what is suppose to happen.

9 **Look over past evaluations.** If you are repeating an event this year that you did last year, how can it be improved? What worked and what didn't work? Form a youth committee for evaluation purposes after each event so next time it rolls around you will be prepared. It will probably cut the planning time in half.

10 **Plan with the teens in mind.** Do you plan events for the teens betterment, or because you think it will be cool? Have you ever met a youth minister who had a great time at the event they planned, but the group hated it? That might be because the guy did what he wanted, and not what the teens wanted. Things that are safe for you may not be safe for the teen. Things that are fun to you may not be fun to the teen. Use good judgement while planning by thinking from the teen perspective.

THIRTY

10 Techniques for Sharing Time with your Family

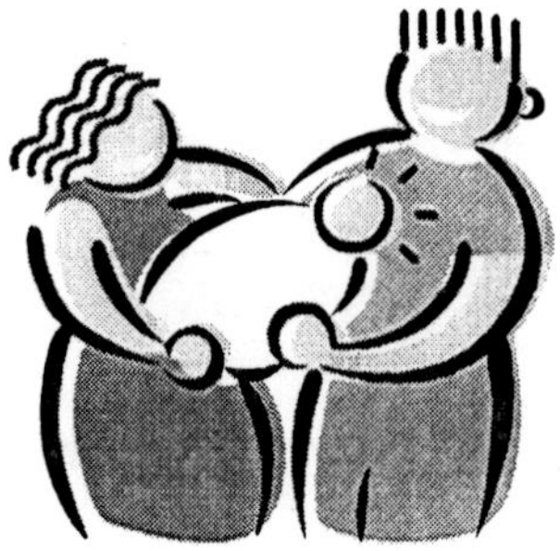

1 **Family Vacation.** At the beginning of each year, go ahead and mark the vacation days you want to take with your family. Check with your spouse and kids to be sure there are no conflicts with other events already on the calendar.

Make this vacation a special time with no ministry interruptions. Don't take any books to read (besides the Bible). Don't take any lessons to work on. Dedicate the vacation solely for your family. Whether you get away for a week, three days or only one day, give your family your complete attention.

2 **Den camping.** Who says you have to leave home for a great time. Not only is den camping fun, but it's also inexpensive. Pick a night of the week and throw some sleeping bags in your living room floor. Anchor a bed sheet between a few chairs to make a tent. Play board games, drink hot chocolate, eat pop corn, wrestle, do whatever you want while camping out within the comfort of your own home. Don't even consider turning on the television or renting a movie. Your kids will love den camping until they reach junior high, at which point you can invite their friends over and show them some of your den camping video footage!

3 **Day in the park.** Here's an activity to do with your kids that you've probably already done, but don't do enough. Head to

your local park and let the little tykes play till they fall over from exhaustion. Slide and swing with them. Spin on the merry-go-round until you all stagger. Have a blast playing like a kid with your kids.

4 **Picnic.** Pack a lunch or load your grill for a cookout. Find a nice spot around a pond and spend the day eating and sharing favorite family memories on a checkered blanket. Bring along your family photo album or old school yearbooks to relive the "good-ole-days."

5 **Camping.** Since you've had a lot of practice in the den, it's time to move outdoors. Camping is not only fun, it's a great teaching tool that relies on cooperation for everything to run smoothly. Here are some things you'll need to consider before getting back to nature.

- Facilities. Do you want to rough it? Have bathrooms available? Take a camper?
- Food. Do you want to stay near a city so you can eat out, or do you want to take all your food?
- Fun. What options will you have when you get there? Does the camp ground offer volleyball, boating, or horseback riding?
- First-aid. Take supplies in case of an accident.
- Weather. What will the temperature be at night? What kind of clothing will you need to pack?

Have an awesome time in the wild enjoying God's creation.

6 **Sports activities.** If your children play sports, support them as a family. If you are the one who plays, ask your family to come out and support you.

Maybe no one in your household participates in sports, but you love to watch them. Take your family to see the local sports team you cheer for and scream and shout as a family.

7 **Benevolence projects.** Call a soup kitchen in your area and ask if your family can come and help serve. Dedicate a day to organizing your church's benevolence room. Adopt a child from a children's home to visit once a month. Adopt a family for Thanksgiving and provide a meal for them or invite

them to your home for the holiday. Pick up trash in your neighborhood. Visit church members in the nursing homes. The options are almost limitless. Don't worry about what you do, just enjoy the blessing of serving as a family.

8 **Mission trip.** Another option for a family vacation is taking a mission trip as a family. Your congregation probably has resources to get you in touch with different missionary organizations if you do not sponsor a missionary yourself. Dedicate yourself to the same missionary effort each year, or go to a new location each year. Your family will get to tell others about Jesus and learn to appreciate the things God has given them.

9 **Hiking and biking.** Lace up your shoes and hit the trails. Spend a day climbing and riding together in a state park or other public land. Listen to the birds as they sing of their creator. Feel the breeze and let it remind you of God's Spirit. Smell the flowers and share the ways that your lives go up as an aroma before God. See the trees and talk about the cross.

10 **Relax.** Take off your watches and forget about time for a while. Watch a movie. Play in the yard. Get out a deck of cards or a board game. In a day where the calendar and clock rule our lives, set aside time specifically for forgetting about time.

Though these ideas are simple they are memory makers. It's often the easy, not the extravagant, that make the biggest impressions on our lives. You will never regret spending too much time with family, but you will regret spending too little time with family.

THIRTY ONE

10 NEEDS OF TEENS

1 Spiritual Needs. "Let us make man in our own image" (Genesis 1:26). From the beginning an inner need for spirituality was given to us by our heavenly parents. There is no time this need can be touched greater than during the teen years. Statistics show that 80% of those who come to saving faith in Jesus do so between the ages of 13 and 19.

In ministry you know that each teen is unique and each maturity level in Christ is unique as well. Yet it is our calling to equip these young believers until they are complete in Christ (Ephesians 4:11). Some may need spiritual milk, while others need a t-bone. Develop strong relationships with your teens and you will learn how to feed them properly.

2 Physical Needs. "Do you not know that your body is the temple of the Holy Spirit, who is in you, whom you have received from God? You are not your own; you were bought with a price, therefore honor God with your body" (I Corinthians 6:19). Teach your group to take care of and honor their bodies. That may mean you offer a class on nutrition. It definitely means teaching a class about sexual purity.

Another physical aspect to be sensitive to during adolescence is the changing of the body. Seventh graders look and act tremendously different from seniors. Some in your group grew beards in the fifth grade, while others forced a peach fuzz goatee in the tenth. Stress the importance of each person being created in God's image, and that all people mature at different rates.

3 Social Needs. God's prophet Elijah lamented, "I am the only one left" (I Kings 19:10). If a prophet needed other people, you can be sure that teens do. When you trace a teen's behavior, it usually comes down to acceptance. They want their peer's approval. Why do they drink? To fit in. Why do they smoke? To look cool with their group. Provide a place for your youth members to fit in that has no prerequisites. Let teens know that they can be cool, or a geek, popular, or unknown, strong, or struggling. Give teens a safe place to fulfill their social needs while being themselves.

4 Intellectual Needs. "The fear of the Lord is the beginning of knowledge, but fools despise wisdom and discipline" (Proverbs 1:7). Help your teens develop in this area by challenging their critical thinking skills. Be like Jesus and tell a parable and don't give the interpretation. Let the group figure it out. When you complete a service project ask the group to go to God's word and find two passages that were fulfilled as a result of their work.

5 Individual Needs. "You created my inmost being; you knit me together in my mother's womb. I praise you because I am fearfully and wonderfully made" (Psalm 139:13-14). King David's esteem didn't come from self, it came from God.

As mentioned earlier, each teen is unique. Unfortunately, each teen usually wants to be like someone else. Ask a youth group, "If you could change one thing about yourself, what would it be?" Someone will raise their hand and say, "Do we have to limit it to one thing?" Help your teens develop God-esteem, not self-esteem.

6 Emotional Needs. "Jesus wept" (John 11:35). From the shortest verse in the Bible we learn about God's feelings. And since we are made in His image we also learn about our feelings. You've learned from experience that teens are on an emotional roller coaster. Make their ride smoother by giving them support, leading classes that help them deal with emotions, and by loving them no matter how emotional they get.

7 Cultural Needs. "When you enter a town and are welcomed, eat what is set before you" (Luke 10:8). At the risk of sounding old fashioned, teach your group good manners. Let them know that on a mission trip that it insults the host not to eat their food. Sure, the teens may not have a taste for fried iguana, but they could develop one over the course of the trip. Another way to meet the cultural need through the church is to experience different worship practices within your fellowship. Attend a predominately Asian, white, black, or other ethnic group's church different from your own. This will allow your teens to understand why God uses so many different churches, and it will make them more aware of their own culture.

8. **Relational Needs.** "Greater love has no man than this, that he lay down his life for his friends" (John 15:13). Fill in the blank: To get friends, you have to ______________. Another way to put that is, "If you go into the world looking for friends, you'll find few. But if you go into the world to be a friend, you'll discover more than you can handle."

You don't have a teen in your group who doesn't want friends. Focus on this need by eliminating any cliques in your ministry, and making sure no one is left out or ignored.

9. **Recreational Needs.** "By the seventh day God had finished the work he had been doing; so on the seventh day he rested from all his work" (Genesis 2:2). God made the seventh day holy for his people to rest. There are times when teens need to be submerged in the spiritual depths, and times when they need to play. Keep a balance in your group by providing plenty of both.

10. **Directional Needs.** "Thomas said to him, 'Lord, we don't know where you are going, so how can we know the way?'" (John 14:5). Does that sound like some teens you know? Jesus showed the twelve the way, so we need to show those we minister to the way as well. Keep Christ as the directional focal point. Teach teens to let every step be taken toward Jesus.

THIRTY TWO

10 Keys for Communication with Teens

1 **Start fresh.** Step before your teens and lay your commitment to them on the line. Make a statement that lets them know that you will give them attention when they speak to you. Tell them that any mistakes you have made communicating in the past are in the past for good. Why start fresh like this? Because we all have trouble communicating in some ways. Some of us talk too much. Others get diverted easily. Maybe we look like we are in a hurry or not interested when a teen is trying to speak with us.

By standing before your group and making a bold statement like this you say to them that, number one, you know you have made mistakes, and, number two, you are willing to do whatever is necessary to mend the communication lines. To prove it, you have a room full of young people who will love to keep you accountable.

2 **Keep secrets.** Confidentiality is important not only in counseling but also in casual conversation. Betsy won't like it when her parents say, "Youth Pastor Pete just told us about how sweet it was that you asked him about a couple of guys in the group that you're wanting to date."

Get permission from the teen to repeat what was said to you. Referring to your conversations in class for an illustration may seem fine to you, but it might embarrass a teen. It's amazing the number of things teens will say for your ears only, that to you may seem like no big deal. Almost everything is a big deal to a teen.

3 **Pick up on non-verbal communication.** "How's it going, Rita?" "Fine," Rita replies with slumped shoulders and tears in her eyes. Think she might not be doing "fine"? Read the "in-between" line language that comes from a roll of the eyes or quick shrug.

Nervousness might be an issue if a teen bites their nails while trying to answer you. Little eye contact might signal a lack of honesty. Don't over interpret these non-verbal communications, just don't neglect them.

4 **Be honest.** Never lie to a teen (or anyone else for that matter). Being cynical by nature, most teens think adults are lying as much as adults think teens are lying.

If a teen catches you in a lie, it gives them an opportunity to not trust you in all areas and that includes Bible class. A teen goes home after devotional. Her parents ask, "What did you learn at devo tonight?" She replies, "Who knows what to believe when he opens his mouth?"

Tell the truth, the whole truth, and nothing but the truth so help you God. Even if it makes you look bad.

5 **What?** Try the following the next time a member of your group wants to share something with you. Give a blank stare and say, "Uuuuh, could you repeat that?"

Write four things here that you believe a response like that would say to a teen.

1.____
2.____
3.____
4.____

Listening to a teen may mean more to them than anything you ever say.

6 **Start the conversation.** Teens can mumble on the phone for hours, but they may find it difficult to talk to their minister. Open the door for them by talking with them when their friends aren't around. If you know of a struggle they have been through recently, ask about the way they are dealing with it.

Be casual and light. Let the teen take the conversation deep if they want. Tell a joke. Bring up your most embarrassing moment. Talk about the first time you remember seeing a VCR, or 286 computers with a whopping 20 meg hard drive that seemed bottomless.

7 Show teens you trust them. I'll never forget an experience at camp in 4th grade. I went to the medical hut because of some poison ivy I played in without knowing. When I told the nurse about it she said, "I don't believe you. I think you got in it because you want to go home." (I would have dove in the ivy earlier if I had known home was in the picture.) Anyway, I wouldn't go back to that nurse if I had a rash the size of Texas. Why? We don't like or talk to people who don't trust us. Teens are the same.

8 Be consistent. Keep your emotions in check and try to speak to teens in a good spirit. If Jack comes by the office after school on Monday and you talk like best friends, then he returns on Thursday and you talk like second cousins twice removed, Jack might remove himself from the picture. If you're having a bad day, let the teen know. Don't kill communication by keeping your group guessing about your mood.

9 Forgive and forget. Once you resolve a problem with a teen, let it go. Never say, "I remember when you...." Never bring up a hurtful situation when you're angry.

A way to keep this in check is simple. Think about all the things you have said under your breath. Think about all the times you failed to talk to God first when you had a problem. Think of what you consider your worst sin. Think about the...aw, forget about it. God has. Do the same for the teens in your group.

> At times we communicate more by what we don't say than what we do say. Keep an open appearance and posture as you talk with your group members.

10 Love. Even if you can't communicate well with a teen, even if you don't know how to listen well, even if you interrupt, even if you sound like a know it all, love covers a multitude of sins, even poor communication skills.

THIRTY THREE

10 Rules for Disciplining Teens

1 **Set the Rules.** "But...but...but...I didn't know we couldn't water grenade the preacher from the balcony." Set the rules and you won't have to worry about such excuses.

Use a New Testament format rather than an Old Testament one. In the Old Testament it took God several books to give the Israelites their rules, better known as the law. In the New Testament the entire law is summed up in two commands. First, "Love the Lord your God with all your heart, soul, mind and strength." Second is like the first, "Love your neighbor as yourself." Put these two "rules" first in your group and add specific variations that you may need according to the event or activity. Such as: "No water grenading the preacher from the balcony!"

2 **Set the punishment.** I'll have to admit it, the fear of hell kept me out of some trouble growing up. What will be "hell" for your group if they break the rules? Confiscating the CD's that were not allowed to be played? Calling parents after a teen leaves the youth retreat campus? Make sure it's clear and cannot be misinterpreted.

If you make your teens and parents sign a contract before a trip, put the rules and punishment on it together. That way teens won't be shocked about breaking an "unknown rule" and parents won't be shocked about the phone call at 2 a.m.

3 **Make sure the punishment fits the crime.** As you set your rules and the enforcement of them ask, "Is this fair?" It's

not fair to send a teen home from a convention because she chewed gum in the assembly and you specifically said not to chew gum. It is fair to send a teen home for bringing a six pack and getting your smallest junior high student drunk.

4 **Discipline in private, not public.** The damage done to a teen and your relationship with him when you discipline in front of the group is almost irreparable. Teens have a lot of pride and public reprimanding embarrasses them enough to leave the church.

Take the teen to the side and explain the reason for the rule, which is not, "Because I said so." Let's say you've got a kid that thinks it's hilarious to push people in the hotel pool in the middle of February. You could say in front of the group, "You idiot! What kind of person are you!" The teen already answered that by pushing someone in the pool, so pull him to the side and say, "Lee, I know you think its funny, but would you like someone to do that to you? The reason we have this rule is not so you won't have fun, but for protection. The water is cold and somebody could get injured or even die. Do you understand? Don't do it again."

5 **If you mak'em, keep'em.** No one will take your rules seriously if you do not enforce them, or if you are not consistent. So what that it's your favorite teen in the group, if they break a rule, they know what the punishment is because you've already stated it. You don't have to be mean or rude, just be matter-of-fact and back up your standards.

6 **Avoid getting angry.** This one is tough because sometimes we're thrilled to get to carry out the punishment. It feels good at times to say, "I've been looking for someone to make an example of, so thanks for accepting the invitation!" There's always one teen in every group that keeps pushing and pushing until you can't take it anymore.

Use these tips when things get heated:

- Walk away.
- Say, "Give me a few minutes. I don't want to say anything I might regret.
- Never, never, never get physical with a teen, unless they are a threat to you or other teens in the group.
- Pray while taking ten deep breaths

7 **Involve the parents.** Most parents will never need to know about discipline. But if a teen continues to be a problem, or keeps breaking the same rule, talk with the parents. If you have developed strong relationships with the parents of your youth members, this should pose no problem. Although it adds to the pressures of parenting, they appreciate a minister willing to work with them in developing their child's character.

Keeping parents informed about the behavior of their child has another advantage. If they are up to date with their teen's class discipline problems, they'll understand why you won't allow him to go on the mission trip.

8 **Discipline with love.** That sounds odd doesn't it? Not from God's perspective. "...the Lord disciplines those he loves, and he punishes everyone he accepts as a son" (Hebrews 12:6). Discipline is not for "teaching a lesson," but for shaping and molding. Explain that to your group. If they can't understand why you are so strict, take a look at discipline from a biblical perspective and help them understand God's principles. You might consider the following verses in your study: Hebrews 12:1-12; Deuteronomy 10:12-13; Proverbs 13:24; 15:5; 23:13-14.

9 **Don't get caught in a power struggle.** It's not about you winning or losing. When the rules are stated and the punishments are set, win and lose don't exist. You didn't punish the teen. Because he knew the rules and broke them, he punished himself. Take personalities out of the picture.

If you have a power struggle in front of the group, you may say or do something that you wouldn't ordinarily because of the pressure. If a teen tries to make you look as bad as possible, keep your cool and remember #4 in this list.

10 **Keep your rules updated.** In 1940, the biggest threat in schools was talking in class. Today it's drugs and guns. If the rules had not changed, our schools would be even less safe. Once a year review your ministry's disciplinary techniques and determine which should stay, which should go, and what new rules need to be implemented.

THIRTY FOUR

10 Tips for Your First Year at a Church

1 **Establish credibility with the entire congregation.** The congregation may see you as the "youth minister" and expect you to be distant from the rest of the people.

- During the first year meet as many people as possible.
- Get to services early and shake hands.
- Remember names and faces not only through personal introductions, but use the picture directory if your church has one.
- Be visible in many roles besides youth. Help serve when your church has a fellowship meal. Drop by the ladies' Tuesday basket weaving group and say hello.

2 **Develop the trust of the leaders.** Focus especially on the elder or deacon that may have acted skeptical about hiring you.

- No surprises. Be up-front with your plans. If the leadership thinks you are trying to be sneaky, you may never gain their trust.
- Form spiritual relationships. It can happen that all encounters with the leadership turn into business meetings. Initiate prayer times, or theological discussions.
- Care and ask about their spiritual well-being. Let the leaders know that you were hired to minister to youth, but you are called to minister to all.
- Support them. Never talk down to, or about, a leader. Give them your love and support, and you will get the same in return. You reap what you sow.

3 **Establish yourself with the parents and teens.** A majority of your time will be spent with these folks, so put a premium on getting to know them from the inside out.

- You will get to know the congregation and leaders on a casual level. Get to know your parents and teens on a personal level.
- Be up front about your goal to develop their entire family spiritually.

4 **Have a dream and vision meeting.** Soon after you arrive at your new congregation, set a date for all the youth and parents to meet together.

- Spell out your rules and expectations.
- Gather family information such as birthdays, emails, addresses, schools attended, etc.
- Hand out a "dreams and goals" sheet for each family to find out what they think God can do through this ministry.
- Express your personal dreams and goals.

5 **Be like Jesus.** Let others see the King living in you and through you.

Write your favorite attributes of Jesus here:______________

____

Write about the attributes of Jesus you have difficulty living:

____

____

Continue to let God transform you into the image of His Son, and allow others to see that transformation taking place.

6 **Be spiritually disciplined.** #5 will not be as difficult if you keep spiritual habits as a priority. These include, but are not limited to the following:

- Bible Study
- Prayer
- Worship
- Evangelism
- Serving
- Stewardship
- Fasting
- Silence and solitude
- Journaling
- Learning

7 **Develop a spiritually strong group.** Within the first year you will discover those who have a relationship with the Lord, those in the group who are faking it, and those barely making it.

- Be dedicated to developing the spiritual aspects of the group and let them know it.
- Plan activities with a purpose.
- Establish student leaders who will help encourage those who are weak in the group.

8 **Meet with each teen individually.** If you don't do this the first year, there will be teens that move out of your group and you may never know they were there.

- Ask about their spiritual life.
- Talk about their dreams and fears.
- Be a friend.
- Give them your home phone number and let them know you are available 24 hours a day for them.

9 **Get into each family's home.** Call every family the first month and set up a time over the next year to visit in their home. Send a card two weeks before the date to remind them of your visit. Getting into their home does several things.

- It shows you are willing to meet on their terms and not yours.
- They feel in control because it is their space.
- They will feel more inclined to say what is on their hearts.
- You will get to see the atmosphere a teen is being raised in, and it may provide clues to any problems, or explain why they have it so together.
- It shows you care.

10 **Be genuine and honest.** Pour out your heart to your people by being transparent.

- Always be you.
- Never wear a mask.
- Always be truthful.
- Never deceive.

THIRTY FIVE

10 ?'s to Ask Adult Volunteer Leaders

1 "Do you love teens and possess a strong desire to minister to them?" You would think that a person who applies for a volunteer position would love teens, but some adults like to be pushy and teens are the easiest people for them to push around. Watch out for people who say, "I think most parents are making major mistakes, and I want to help this group tow the line the way it's supposed to be done." Any person who acts heavy handed during an interview will be even heavier with the group.

Let Mr. Heavy go his way and look for adults who speak from their hearts about the difficulties teens face, and the promise that each of them has within.

2 "What type of spiritual role model do you feel you would be to the teens?" You need someone who can do more than corral the group when it's time to meet back at the bus. Invite adults to join the group who are set on helping teens become surrendered followers of Jesus. They should talk about their personal devotional habits. If they don't, then ask them if they are in the Word consistently, memorize scripture, fasting, praying, etc. A person who is not a disciple of Christ in these elementary ways will have difficulty aiding in the maturing of your group in these same areas.

3 "Do you believe God will work through you in this ministry?" As He did in the Bible, God still uses people today to do His will. Many people have low self-confidence, and low God confidence. They think so little of themselves that they can't believe God would use them for anything. The truth is that God uses all believers for His purposes. Those who feel God has called them to minister in the youth area must believe that the Lord will use them to do things beyond their ability.

4 **"How will you respond to a teen who calls you at midnight needing to talk about a problem?"** Most teens will call you, but as they develop relationships with the volunteers, they may feel close enough to call at midnight.

Volunteers should respond by listening and offering to do what is needed according to the situation. If the teen is in trouble then the volunteer needs to contact the teen's parents, or authorities if needed. Beware of the prospective volunteer who says, "I'd tell them to call back in the morning."

5 **"How would you go about building relationships with the teens?"** This will allow you to determine if this person has thought about what it takes to form friendships with teens. Will he baby them? Will she put them in a seating arrangement to learn their names?

Look for someone who is willing to spend time with teens outside of planned activities, and will love them unconditionally.

> *Asking tough questions doesn't come naturally for most of us. Yet, when we ask these types of questions we find that future results contain more blessings than if we fail to ask.*

6 **"Can you be yourself around teens?"** Encourage all volunteers to be who God designed and gifted them to be. They don't have to be able to pull a rabbit from a hat. They don't have to be impressive.

The Lord placed each person in the body just as He desired (I Cor. 12:18). The truth is that a pinkie volunteer needs to be a pinkie, not a hand. An eye volunteer needs to be an eye and not a nose. Teens appreciate authenticity more than impressibility.

7 **"How much time will you be able to devote to this ministry?"** Some volunteers may have an hour a week, while others may have fifteen hours. Assign their ministry responsibilities according to the amount of time they have available. You may find that your most gifted volunteer has the least amount of time to contribute, which may mean that your least gifted with the most time gets the task that requires the most hours.

Be up-front about the amount of time required for the ministry your volunteers desire. If they get halfway through the project and realize they don't have enough time, you will be the one to complete it.

8 "Can you be open and honest with the teens and your co-ministry leaders?" Honest means that the volunteer will decline jobs they can't handle. It means they are willing to take the responsibility for their mistakes. Honesty means they will be who they are and not try to appear as more or less than that.

Honesty does not mean being brutally honest and insensitive. It is not a "tell it like it is" attitude. Honesty is openness that comes from a humble spirit that works for the good of others and not self.

9 "Will you refer teens to someone else if you cannot help them with a specific problem?" Beware of the "know-it-all" volunteer who has all the answers. That dangerous breed of ministry leader will give an ill-advised solution before admitting to not knowing something.

Supply your volunteers with a list of phone numbers to call when a teen needs help. Provide numbers in case a teen has a spiritual need, substance abuse problem, suicidal threats, psychological need, etc. Contact the people and make sure it is alright to recommend them. Also, tell volunteers to use these numbers infrequently.

10 "What is the strongest asset you will bring to this ministry?" Designate your volunteers toward a ministry that involves their strengths. An athletic volunteer may not be the best choice for Bake-n-Take day. A yard maintenance volunteer would probably have difficulty helping teens develop the youth web page. That's not to say that people can't crossover to be used in various areas. But using people according to their strengths will allow your ministries to run more efficiently.

THIRTY SIX

10 Teen Characteristics

1 Teens want to feel loved and accepted. When it comes to these two things, teens are no different from the rest of us. We all want to feel loved. We all want to be accepted based on who we are, not what others want us to be.

Focus on the uniqueness of each individual. Don't tease a teen about their clothing, or seemingly strange hair style. Show unconditional love to each teen without showing favoritism.

2 Teens want solid spiritual roles models. Parents remain the number one source of spiritual guidance according to teenagers. Youth ministers rank second.

Teens want more than talk, they want to see us living the things we teach in class. The old saying is true, "I'd rather see a sermon than hear one any day." When we and parents develop spiritual habits, authentic lives, and genuine compassion for others, teens will recognize it and want the same for their lives. If, however, they see us and their parents talk about a life of integrity before God, yet show little desire for that in our personal lives, they'll learn that Christianity is more about looking good than living good.

While you and their parents occupy the top two spots in the influence category, don't forget to put other strong role models in front of your group. Invite new borns in Christ to share their excitement. Ask some of your elderly members to tell about what it takes to live for Jesus over the long haul. Keep a variety of faces in front of your group so they'll know you're not the only Christian they know.

3 Teens can be greatly used by God. David and Daniel are two Bible teens that come to mind when thinking about biblical young people used by God. Teens today may think that David and Daniel were used by God "back then" and that they could never be used by God like that. Here are a few ways God can use teens today that adults will have a harder time with:

- Teens can reach people in their own age group more effectively than adults.
- Teens can use sports, clubs, cheerleading, etc. as ways to impact a large number of people for Christ in a short amount of time.
- Most teens are not "set in their ways" and play a literal role in changing the lives of people their age forever.

4 Teens can be rebellious. A teen being rebellious is a teen being...well...him or herself. Blame it on hormones, a poor home life, or Adam and Eve in the garden, teens wrestle with authority. They want to be considered adults without the bills or headaches. There are many things they want to do without any restrictions. They think curfew is for elementary kids, and chaperones are for sissies. Teens want to be tough, but able to crawl into mama's lap when they get hurt. They feel caught in a twilight zone between being a kid and being an adult and the only way they know to retaliate is to rebel.

When teens rebel, try not to take it personally. Remain calm, it usually has nothing to do with you or your ministry. It has everything to do with "Nobody understands," "I can't wait till I get out of this dump and don't have to come back!" "I don't care what you say. Cheryl and I are getting married." In light of those rebellious comments and the other thousand you have heard, be patient and love the teens through their rebellious stage.

5 Teens want discipline. It's a well kept secret that teens actually want rules. Some want their parents to keep them from the party, so they won't feel the pressure to drink. Teens do appreciate their parents standing by their word even if it means they won't get their way. Of course, most of this isn't realized for another ten years. But then they'll thank you.

6 Teens are not easily motivated - unless it's their idea. Most teens want to do what they want when they want. Dad can ask them to take out the trash and they will, "After this show goes off." Take a lesson from Tom Sawyer. He got everyone to help him white wash a fence my making them feel like it was the best thing that could happen to them. Motivate teens by: 1) Showing your enthusiasm. 2) Letting them know up front what they will achieve from the activity. 3) Using ideas that they generate. They may not be motivated to do what you want, but they love doing what they want.

7 **Teens are very impressionable.** Teens may say they want to be different, to be an individual, but millions of Air Jordan basketball shoes prove otherwise.

Teens pick up on our expressions and may adopt them. They notice the way someone walks or talks that they admire and they begin walking and talking that way. In high school we always knew who played sports by their strut. Nobody walks like that by nature. Teens had to pick it up from somebody else. Use this characteristic as a tool to mold teens, and as a guard for your own life in front of them.

8 **Teens struggle with and for independence.** Teens long for adult responsibility but want to do things their way. Translation: Be ready to pick them up when they fail and fall, and let them know that failure is part of growing, but not part of them personally. Provide ways for teens to increase their independence through ministry. Give them your availability when they need help, but stand back and let them go it alone when they don't net support.

9 **Teens wrestle with stress, peer pressure and temptation.** Many adults see the teen years as carefree, but teens don't see it that way. They feel the pressure of making the grades without appearing too smart. They want to be accepted and do the cool thing without getting caught. They are willing to go to almost any length to fit in and feel the love of their peers. Develop a support ministry where your teens rely on each other for strength to survive.

10 **Teens want to know adults care about them.** No amount of programs can take the place of caring. Teens want relationships more than anything else. We all do.

THIRTY SEVEN

10 Techniques for Reaching Troubled Teens

1 **Love the unloved.** In Luke 7 a "sinful woman" entered the house of Simon the Pharisee to anointed the feet of Jesus. Simon couldn't believe that Jesus would allow her to touch Him. Reading Simon's thoughts Jesus said to him, "Her many sins have been forgiven - for she loved much. But he who has been forgiven little loves little."

The "unchurched" may feel like the woman at Simon's house, and we have the same two options. First, we can be like the Pharisee and refuse to get our life dirty. Or, we can be like Jesus and love the unloved. We may find that those troubled teens can become the greatest lovers in our group because much has been forgiven.

2 **Let God work.** "No one can come to me unless the Father who sent me draws him" (John 6:44). It's God's transforming power that turns teens around. We need to be God's instruments as He draws young people to Him. When we try to do God's work for Him we end up drawing teens toward us and away from the Master.

Watch for God's direction and allow Him to lead you toward the right approach with each teen.

3 **Let teens witness your transformation.** "Now the Lord is the Spirit and where the Spirit of the Lord is there is freedom. And we, who with unveiled faces all reflect the Lord's glory, are being transformed into his likeness with ever increasing glory, which comes from the Lord, who is the Spirit" (II Cor. 3:17-18). Our transforming glory in Christ is "ever increasing." That means that teens can see the ongoing

changes in our lives by God. Young people who are struggling can gain strength knowing that becoming like Christ is a process, not a one time event. If our walk with Christ does not continue to mature us troubled teens may not look to the Lord because they may think our lives are all there is to Christianity. But if we are allowing God to continue His work in and through us, teens will see it and be drawn to God through our changed lives.

4 **Pray with and for them.** When a teen asks, "Could you put this on your prayer list?" Pray with him or her immediately concerning the request and promise that you will continue to pray about it.

Acts 2:42 says that the first believers, "devoted themselves...to prayer." Prayer reaffirms number two on this list; you are letting God work. It gives assurance to teens because they may not feel like God listens to their prayers, but for some reason they believe God will listen to yours.

5 **Study the Word with them.** "For the word of God is living and active. Sharper than any double-edged sword, it penetrates even to dividing soul and spirit, joints and marrow; it judges the thoughts and attitudes of the heart" (Hebrews 4:12). Let God's Word do the work. Sit down with the teens and study together to discover what God says about their situation.

A teen who is failing sexually may believe what we tell him/her regarding sexual sin, but that can't impact them like reading what God has to say on the subject. Guide teens through a study by supplying the passages and allowing the teen to interpret what it means. That way the teen discovers the truth for himself.

6 **Discover their coveted relationships.** "Jonathan became one in spirit with David, and he loved him as himself" (I Samuel 18:1). You may not be able to reach every teen, but most probably have someone in his life herespects. If you have a troubled teen who refuses to let down her life barriers, find out who she will listen to. Talk with that person, tell them what you know about the situation, and ask for their help. We can't let pride get in the way of reaching a teen. We've got to admit that to help the teens that don't like us, or don't trust us, we've got to dig deep and discover another way to assist.

7 Concentrate on teens' good traits. "Finally, brothers, whatever is true, whatever is noble, whatever is right, whatever is pure, whatever is lovely, whatever is admirable—if anything is excellent or praiseworthy—think about such things" (Philippians 4:8). For some in our group this might be a task, but it can be done. Think about the "worst" teen in your group. Now, what is praiseworthy about that person? What is admirable about him/her? Teens know enough negative aspects about themselves without us giving them more. The more positives we can find in teens the more likely we can reach them.

8 Put yourself in their shoes. "If someone forces you to go one mile, go with him two miles" (Matthew 5:41). When we walk a mile in a teen's shoes we can better relate. We faced some of the same struggles when we were teens, but not on the level that today's young people face. Get on their side of the fence by trying to understand their problems, not by belittling them. If a teen comes to you and their life's crisis is a hurricane to them, but a gentle shower to you, put yourself in their shoes. Look at it from their perspective, and reach out with care.

9 Be gentle, but firm. "My son, do not make light of the Lord's discipline, and do not lose heart when he rebukes you, because the Lord disciplines those he loves, and he punishes everyone he accepts as a son" (Hebrews 12:5b-6). When the Lord disciplines us, He is serious about it, but He doesn't want us to get so overwhelmed by it that we can't go on.

Teens are going to get in trouble and discipline is part of the process. We should discipline the way the Lord disciplines us. It's gentle, but firm. It makes a point, but doesn't leave us exasperated.

10 Be patient. "Better a patient man than a warrior, a man who controls his temper than one who takes a city" (Proverbs 16:32). Take your time when helping troubled teens. Their problems didn't develop over night, and the solutions won't come over night. Invest time in teens according to their individual needs.

THIRTY EIGHT

10 Tools for Times of Crisis

1 **Ask for guidance.** As in any area of life, don't try to go it alone. Seek the counsel of two major influences. First, ask God for His guidance. No crisis surprises Him with its complexities. No crisis is so great that God can't overcome it. Ask the Lord to reveal the correct direction, and the best solution for the dilemma.

After talking with God, talk with someone who you know has been through a similar crisis. The solution that worked for that person may work for you. Call other youthworkers and find out if they have any teens facing a similar struggle, and ask how they are dealing with it.

2 **Face the crisis head-on.** Closing our eyes and hoping the storm will pass isn't the best solution. When we fail to meet the problem head-on, or worse, pretend it doesn't exist, the situation intensifies and more people end up hurt.

The steps taken depend on the situation. If a girl is pregnant in your group and is afraid to tell her parents, you may need to intercede for her. If one of your senior guys blows his university scholarship by driving while drunk, you may have to help him get counseling and vouch for his character. Nothing about getting involved with someone's crisis is pleasant, but as ministers we are called to help mend the broken.

3 **Attack the problem, never the person.** "Love the sinner, hate the sin." People's problems are personal to them. It is difficult for individuals to separate our comments about their behavior from comments about them. To prevent teens from getting the idea that you are attacking or condemning them, use terms that distinguish their problem from their person. Never say, "You are a liar, and always have been." Instead say, "Lying never solves the problem, does it? What are some ways that lying has caused the problems in your life." There is a difference is calling a teen a liar, and admitting that they have a sin problem with lying. This isn't to lessen the crisis, but to keep the individual from being impossible to reach because of their negative esteem.

4 **Handle it now, don't hesitate.** Procrastination only makes a crisis swell. Tackling a problem quickly can help contain the crisis and allow it to be solved before it gets out of hand (even more so than it may already be). After a tough day it's so much easier to say, "I'll call Jack tomorrow about the fight with his parents." What may be a few hours to us can feel like a year to a teen. Put crisis situations as top priority so teens will know they can depend on you when they hurt.

5 **Stay Calm.** On every flight the stewards give the "in case of an emergency" instructions. If the cabin loses pressure an oxygen mask will drop down, place it securely around your head. In case of a water landing - better known as a crash - your seat can be turned into a floatation device. But the key for the success of these emergency instructions it that the passengers remain calm. When everyone is screaming, no one gets the mask on, or the seat properly adjusted for floating. The same is true when encountering any crisis. If a teen comes and tells you about his drug habit, overreacting will not be the course to pursue. Don't cover your face with your hand, moan, and lament, "How? How? How? How could it be you? Of all the people in the group, how could it be you?" The teen may have thought they could get through the problem relatively easy, but now you have convinced him that he may never recover. Stay calm, get all the facts and work toward the solution.

6 **Turn to others for help.** Using the above example, let's say that the drug habit turns out to be serious abuse. If we are not licensed or otherwise qualified to give professional help, get in contact with those who are.

7 **Take it one day at a time.** Some problems may be solved with a few words, others may take weeks. We may have a teen that requires a personal call or meeting on a daily basis for a while until he or she can get through the crisis. Some teens may need a weekly note to let them know you are thinking and praying for them.

Don't forget that the Son shines after every storm.

8 **"Remember, you're not alone."** The notes or calls you make according to #7 lets teens know they are not alone. We may not feel what they feel, or hurt like they hurt, but they will know we are present for their pain. We may feel that our words, cards, or pats on the back don't mean that much because they don't cost much, but teens don't forget it. We need to constantly show that we are there for them no matter how small it may appear to us.

9 **Count the blessings.** During a crisis it is tough for anyone to see the light at the end of the tunnel, or the silver lining in the cloud. Challenge each person you work with to continue to see the positives in light of the overwhelming negatives. If a teen says, "I can't think of one good thing in my life right now," ask where they slept last night. Ask about the clothes they wear, or the food they eat. Sound ridiculous? It only points to the truth that we take most things for granted, especially our blessings. By being thankful for the daily necessities, teens may discover that they have everything they need, but their crisis is about what they want.

10 **Let it go.** When it's over, it's over. Forget about it.

THIRTY NINE

10 Tips for Getting a Raise

According to our studies numbers 1 and 10 might actually work. Use the others at your own risk!

1 **Do your job.** Most of us like to use the term "ministry," but when you get down to it, we get paid to do a job. Our job happens to be working with teens, while another's occupation may be brain surgery (those two sound oddly similar).

In the non-ministry related work force people get raises based on the cost of living, performance or promotion. Since most churches don't know what it cost to live - as evidenced by our salaries - and promotions are only received by moving to another church, let's consider performance as the best way to get a raise. Don't worry, we won't have to work harder, just smarter. Do this by staying close to the parents and becoming their friend. Go the second mile with your teens. Keep the leadership posted on everything you do. Prove to them that they got a deal when they got you at such a low paying package, then when your review comes up you'll be in a good position to get a raise.

2 **Wear clothes from your grandfather's clothes trunk from World War II.** The reason? Mothballs. Nothing shares the "I'm in need" smell better than mothballs. Here are some more keys to clothing success: Make sure your pant's legs are too short and uneven. Your shirt should be polyester, and the tie cannot, must not, match. And even though it was packed in mothballs, there should be a few holes in the coat. Oops, sorry for being politically incorrect. Ladies, your grandfather's suit may be too much, so get your grandmother's old dress -

they tend to hold the mothball aroma better anyway.

3 **Drive an old car.** Have you ever heard a car that sounded like it had the flu when it was started? Well, that's exactly what you want. If it doesn't have enough dents, borrow a sledge hammer from your next door neighbor. If it doesn't have enough dirt, ask the kids that live around you to have a mud fight with your car placed strategically in the middle. Also, smoke flooding out the tail pipe as you drive into the church parking lot will help get your point across.

4 **Get caught grocery shopping in the benevolent food pantry.** If your church gives food to the needy, consider yourself lucky. It will be difficult for the church not to give you a raise as you're caught (this must happen) while "grocery shopping." Ask for their help to fill your bag and show them the shopping list made out in your spouse's handwriting.

5 **Compare salaries with custodians.** As your church leaders walk in your office, be on the phone talking to a fellow minister, "Your custodian makes how much?! Do you guys have any openings?" This might be a little low, but shame works as a good tactic most of the time. Can't you hear the conversation in the next leader's meeting, "Did you know that Henry the garbage guy over at XYZ Church makes more than our youth minister? What kind of people are we?"

6 **Inquire about the food stamp program.** Who heads the finance committee in your church? Who is in charge of your raise? Write his or her name here:________________________
Sometime before or after services, preferably with a small crowd assembled, ask about your state's food stamp policy. Ask how to sign up for the program, where to sign up, and how long it will take to get the stamps. When they ask who this is for, look around very embarrassed and say in a most unconvincing voice, "Don't worry, it's not for us. Don't worry about us, we're doing fine. Just...just...just...don't concern yourself, we're getting by."

7 **Moonlight.** Get an application for the night shift at a fast food restaurant close to your church building. Walk by the nosiest secretary on staff because you know she always looks over what you have in your hands when you pass her desk. Fill out the application and leave it on your desk so anyone who enters can see it. For a special touch, fill in the comments section of the application with: DESPERATE - I NEED HELP IMMEDIATELY.

8 **Set up fund raising canisters around the building.** Get several large juice cans, cut a slit in the top (large enough to accept bills and checks), and drain the juice. Wash it out and dry it. While it dries, get some small sheets of paper and a marker and write "Please give to the youth minister relief fund" on each sheet, then glue them to the cans. If possible get a picture of you made in your grandfather's suit or grandmother's dress mentioned in number two and attach it to the can. Place these around the building, predominately in the areas where the rich members frequent.

9 **Ride a bike.** If nothing has worked so far, start riding a bike to work. If members and staff start congratulating you on being so health conscious, tell them your not, you had to sell your car so you could eat. Follow that up by mentioning that you really didn't mind moving out of your house and that the tent you're calling home is working out when it doesn't rain.

10 **Ask for one** If no hints are taken, and no one picks up on what a great job you're doing, break down and ask for a raise. The church may have the money, but is not aware of your needs. Take your household budget with you and seriously explain the financial trouble you are experiencing. In light of all the good suggestions we have given you so far, you may find that you might actually get a raise if you just ask.

FORTY

10 Tips for Helping Teens Develop a Strong Self-Image

1 **Explain "as you love yourself."** With so much talk of humility, most teens think that means to hate yourself. Denying self and hating self are two entirely different things. Explain how God wants teens to "love your neighbor as yourself." Loving self doesn't mean being in love with yourself. It means that we have a good self-image, a God-image. We are important not because of who we are, but *whose* we are.

Teens and adults need to be able to look at their lives and know that as God's children they are priceless to God. Regardless of how others feel about them. Whether the world thinks we're geeks or freaks, weirdoes or wackos, only God's view and vision of us counts. And to Him we are worth the price of His Son hammered to a cross.

2 **Admit your insecurities.** As the youth leader, you may appear larger than life to the teens. They may look at you and think, "I'll never have it together like that." We know the truth. We're not together. We have struggles, bad hair days, and poor complexions at times. When it's appropriate, share with individual teens the things that cause your self-esteem to shrink. Share as well the ways that the Lord strengthens you when you don't feel so hot.

When we open up to our group members, their insecurities will be healed when they know that everyone deals with some low-esteem issues.

3 Encourage self-talk. Tell your teens to stand in front of the mirror every morning and night and repeat, “God don’t make no junk,” or “I’m made in God’s image.” It might sound silly, but we really do believe what we say to ourselves.

Why do some teens feel stupid? Because someone told them they were stupid, or they told themselves. Why do some teens feel ugly? Because someone told them they were ugly, or they told themselves. Encourage your group to reinforce a biblical perception of themselves by talking about how God views them.

4 Help teens challenge themselves. Get your teens proactive in the war against insecurity. A girl might decide that she will stop buying magazines that promote the “perfect look.” A guy might choose to stop listening to music that degrades God’s creation by elevating suicide over life.

In place of those the girl may want to start reading a Christian magazine for young ladies, while the guy might toss out his CD collection and replace it with Christian artists. We are what we absorb, so challenge your teens to challenge themselves!

Every teen wrestles with self-esteem, and most of them get clobbered by it. Develop God-esteem in your group. Do this by constantly reminding them that they are precious and priceless to God. With Him everyone fits in. There are no misfits in the Kingdom.

5 Provide ways for teens to give of themselves. It’s tough to feel sorry for yourself when your eyes are on others. Keep a list of area organizations that use teens for volunteers. Whenever a guy comes into your office looking low and using terms that beat up his emotions, send him down to the area children’s hospital and let him share his life.

If a girl comes in upset about not having the best clothes and how unattractive she feels, call the soup kitchen and arrange an afternoon of service. We often feel bad about ourselves until we are around those who have much less than we do. As teens give of themselves, they will learn more about who God made them to be.

6 **Support teen accountability groups.** Encourage your teens to share their insecurities with the peers they trust. All of us have a low self-esteem about something. Teens will find comfort in knowing that everyone has weaknesses and that they are not alone.

It's critical that these groups be made up of individuals who respect one another. One "cool dude" could blow the whole effort with his insensitivity.

7 **Send teens articles that relate to their struggle.** Most of us can handle a problem more effectively if we understand the problem. If you run across an article called "Beauty is Only Skin Deep" that talks about godliness being more important that looks, cut it out and mail it to those in the group who talk about how ugly they are. If you have some who feel untalented, or unneeded, clip out some articles that talk about Moses being God's chosen, but reluctant, servant.

Be cautious when sharing these articles. Those receiving them could think you agree with their plight. The girl who feels unattractive might think, "She obviously thinks I'm ugly or she wouldn't have sent this story." Be wise in the approach you take.

8 **Help teens remain focused.** Teens may become apathetic or lazy when consumed by a low self-esteem. Help them take their mind off themselves by helping them stay focused. Call and make sure they are up to speed on the term paper due next week. Ask how their record breaking year in basketball is holding up.

9 **"Patience, Grasshopper."** The teacher on Kung Fu always reminded his student to remain patient. No one can master Kung Fu over night, it takes years. Teens won't master their self-esteem over night either. Tell them to remain patient and to allow the Master to shape them in His time.

10 **Help teens identify the problem and be proactive.** Some problems are more mental than physical. Help teens discover the root of the problem and provide a way to overcome it.

FORTY ONE

10 TRIP CHECKPOINTS

1 Determine the cost. Check the prices of hotels, airlines, buses, rentals, fees, etc. Don't let an unforeseen cost hurt the trip or take out the budget. Look in the phonebook and call all the businesses that relate to your activity and compare prices. If possible ride out to their lot and check out the rentals personally to make sure their "good deal" isn't a bad deal for you.

If your planning will require rental away from home, use a travel agent or do your own research online with a company like Travelocity (www.travelocity.com). Companies like these will allow you to compare prices between several companies providing the same service.

2 Acquire all necessary forms and have them signed. What forms are needed for the trip you are taking? Medical release forms? Permission slips? You will want to get signatures, insurance card numbers, and a notary seal in some cases. Check your state laws to determine exactly what forms you need for each trip. If not expressly stated on your form, you will also need emergency phone numbers, medication allergies, and any other information a parent may feel is needed to protect their child in the case of an emergency.

3 Use commitment contracts. Hold teens accountable by specifically stating the do's and don't's of the trip. Make a list of all requirements and have teens and parents sign the contract. This type of commitment will help deter surprises and statements like, "I didn't know it was against the rules to pull the fire alarm at the hotel." A commitment contract lets parents and teens know that trips are not "do what I want" outings.

4 **Check maintenance on all transportation.** This may come as a shock to most of you, but I've actually heard about a few church vans and buses that broke down on a trip. Can you believe it? Even more amazing is that the ministers in fault actually admitted that they didn't get the vehicles checked out before leaving town.

Don't wait until the last minute to get gasoline, oil, tires pumped, etc. Most church vehicles have enough problems to warrant being in the shop for a week, so plan ahead and keep maintenance up to par. We have enough headaches on the trip without having to worry about mechanical problems.

5 **Collect money.** I know most of you couldn't believe that some church vans break down, but I'm going to take a risk and tell you something else you might not believe. Some teens sign up for events and then back out a couple of days before, leaving the church with the bill. To prevent this from happening to you, require teens pay up front before they are allowed to register for an activity or trip. Let it be known that the money is nonrefundable and if a teen drops out, the money is still needed to pay for the spot for which they registered.

6 **Make reservations.** After securing your budget and getting a general count of those attending, reserve any transportation, lodging, etc. you may need. Do this as far in advance as you can so you will be guaranteed what you want. I don't know how many times I wasted half a day

"Suppose one of you wants to build a tower. Will he not first sit down and estimate the cost to see if he has enough money to complete it?" Luke 14:28
Sit down and count out each step before each trip.

looking for luggagc trailers because I failed to reserve one.

Be sure to keep a record of a business' cancellation policy. If something changes and you don't need the extra van or rooms, contact the establishment as possible to avoid unnecessary charges.

7. **Double check the reservations.** A week before the trip, recheck all your reservations and confirmation numbers. All over the country each year youth ministers and volunteers hear the dreaded words, "I'm sorry, but I can't seem to find your reservation. Are you sure you placed it with us?" When making reservations, ask for something in writing to be sent to you so you will have a record.

8. **Provide an itinerary.** Let parents know where you will be each day, which includes expected times of departure and arrivals. Make sure phone numbers for the places you will be staying are given to the parents so they can call in case of emergencies, or just to check on their little darling.

9. **Recruit and organize your chaperones.** Line up those who will we traveling with you well in advance. Most parents and other volunteers need to take off work and will have to make those arrangements early.

10. **Check first aid and emergency kits.** Your state may require you to have these item on board your vehicles. Is the first aid kit well stocked and updated? Is the fire extinguisher regulated? Do you have reflective triangles, or cones for other travelers to see if you have to pull over? Take every safety precaution so an accident or emergency won't become even more severe.

FORTY TWO

10 Tips for Personal Finance

1 **Give God the first fruit from your paycheck.** "Will a man rob God? Yet you rob me. But you ask, 'How do we rob you?' In tithes and offerings (Malichi 3:8). Throughout Scripture God makes it clear that He desires our "first fruits." He deserves our "first fruits." The Lord promises to care for us the way He cares for the birds of the air and lilies of the fields. It's easy to rationalize about our low pay and claim that since God already has so much of our time, He doesn't care about our money. Not true. He cares because He knows how precious it is to us. Our giving reflects how precious He is to us.

2 **Set a simple budget and stick to it.** "Suppose one of you wants to build a tower. Will he not first sit down and estimate the cost to see if he has enough money to complete it?" (Luke 14:28). Without a budget most of us have no idea where our money goes. In fact, most of us have said those exact words, "Where did all the money go?" Five dollars here, ten dollars there, and before we know it all the deneros disappear.

God said that no one builds without counting the cost. Likewise, we need to build financial security into our lives by counting the cost of each month and not going beyond it.

3 **Be careful with credit.** "The wicked borrow and do not repay, but the righteous give generously." (Psalm 27:31). I average one credit card offer per day in my mail box. Of course, every offer is unbelievable. The companies promise to revive my credit rating, give me a large amount of money, with low monthly payments, and assures me that their interest rate is the lowest on the planet. By the time I charge $10,000 worth of items it doesn't matter how low they claim the payment will be, I won't be able to pay it.

Don't get sucked into the credit trap. Pay for everything with cash. If you don't have the money don't get it.

4 **Keep accurate monthly records.** "Again, it will be like a man going on a journey, who called his servants and entrusted his property to them" (Matthew 25:14). Earlier in the book you were challenge to think of time as God's time. Well, think of money as God's money. If the Lord showed up at our homes and asked us to give an account of what we were doing with His funds, would we be able to? Would we be ashamed? Would we apologize and say, "You know, Lord, I've been meaning to take a closer look at that very thing tomorrow?"

5 **Don't allow expenses to exceed income.** "After he had spent everything, there was a severe famine in that whole country, and he began to be in need" (Luke 15:14). The prodigal son learned about expenses exceeding income. He ended up shoveling slop for pigs. We might not wind up in the same position, but repossession could be in the forecast.

6 **Recognize the difference between wants and needs.** "And my God will meet all your needs according to his glorious riches in Christ Jesus" (Philippians 4:19). We all have a wish list as long as the number of rumors floating around the White House. But do we need all of those things? In the margin, make a list of things you need, things you must have in order to survive. Those needs are what God wants us to center on.

A few years ago I heard Charles Stanley teach about giving to the Lord. He mentioned that people like to point out that we are under grace not under the old law with its tithe. Charles responds by saying, "Where does the Bible say that I should do less, be less or give less because I am under grace and not

7 **Save.** “Ants are creatures of little strength, yet they store up their food in the summer;” (Proverbs 30:25). We can learn a lot from ants. Saving prepares us for the future. Emergencies will come. Loss of employment is possible. Where will we be if it happens to us? How will the needs be met?

Even if you can only save $10 a month, do it. Make it a constant goal to increase your savings contributions every quarter until you are putting at least 10% of your income in savings each month. It may seem impossible, but look at the ants, they store up food in the summer because they know winter is coming.

8 **Get advice.** “Plans fail for lack of counsel, but with many advisors they succeed” (Proverbs 17:22). If you are not particularly savvy with money, don’t feel embarrassed to get advice. There may be someone in your congregation who can help you get your finances under control. If not, go to a professional advisor. The money invested in their services will be returned many times in the money you save as a result of following their plan.

9 **Control your money, don’t let it control you.** “For all can see that wise men die; the foolish and the senseless alike perish and leave their wealth to others” (Psalm 49:10). No matter how we horde it, use it, or abuse it, we’re all going to leave it behind. Money and the things it can buy are just temporary, so there’s no need to allow it to control our lives. View money as a tool to do God’s will, not as a temptation to control your life.

10 **Stick with your plan.** “The plans of the diligent lead to profit as surely as haste leads to poverty” (Proverbs 21:5). Impulse spending and like actions will ruin us financially. Whatever rules you establish for your finances, stick with them! The “a few dollars here and there won’t matter” attitude can quickly lead to financial trouble. Stay focused, and place your money and faith in the hands of God.

FORTY THREE

10 Don'ts for Counseling Teens

1 Don't force a teen into counseling. Want a quick way to shut teens down? Make them come to you for counseling. If it's not their idea to come, or at least partially their idea, little will be accomplished. By nature teens like to have control, and when pushed into a corner they feel trapped and unwilling to share.

We need to let teens know that we are available for any problem they may have. Listening to them well in casual conversations will make them more likely to come to us for private consolation. Encourage, but don't force, teens to visit you for counseling if you notice a problem that may call for it.

2 Don't act shocked. If a teen tells you that he has a sexually transmitted disease and he thinks he has given it to three girls, remain calm and resist saying, "You *think*?" Be prepared for anything. A teen may enter your office with anything from suicide to homicide on his or her mind. When we act shocked and give one of those *of all the people, I never would have thought* looks, it makes a teen feel very small.

3 Don't be too professional. Is the office the best place to meet with teens? Perhaps walking around a park would work better, or meeting at a fast food place near their school. If you have a close relationship with a teen, an informal setting may work best. No one likes being called to the office.

Do you wear a tie as part of your daily attire? Ditch it and take off your coat. The more serious you look, the more serious a teen may perceive their problem to be. On the other hand, if you're rubbing tanning lotion on when a teen comes to talk, she may feel that you don't take anything seriously. You'll be professional enough for a teen if you're dressed casually, and tuned into their needs.

4 **Don't act like you have all the answers.** Although 90% of the parents beat down our door during the week looking for solutions, we know we don't have all the solutions. So when a teen comes looking for answers it's OK to say, "I don't know exactly what you should do. Let's give it some thought and get back together in a couple of days." This type of response shows more wisdom than always having a pat answer.

When we act like we have all the answers, or have it all together, teens will close up and refuse to share. Keep an open mind, and be honest about what you can and cannot handle.

5 **Don't treat them differently after a session.** We may get disappointed or get frustrated with a teen but never let it show in public for two reasons. First, the teen probably feels bad enough without you changing your attitude toward him. And if you act strange or distant he may stop coming to counseling and possibly stop attending church. Second, it may cause others in the group to wonder what's wrong with the teen that you would treat him differently. Rumors may start, or the truth may come out, and what a teen wanted to keep silent may become the talk of the group.

6 **Don't expect one session to solve the problem.** Have you ever thought, "I've got thirty minutes to solve Patsy's problem. That ought to be just enough time, then I can get to the club." It takes time to get to know someone and to get someone to open up. It may take several sessions before the root of the problem shows up. Never rush through counseling. Be patient and thorough.

7 **Don't exclude the parents when they are needed.** It's a huge mistake to disregard the feelings of parents when their teens are involved. We minister to aid the parents, not to take their place. We don't have to break confidentiality to let parents know if things are going well. There will be times when parents have little need to know the details because the problem is not serious, or there may be times when specifics need to be shared because a teen's life is in danger. Either way, we don't need to keep parents completely in the dark. Share what you can and reassure them that you are praying for them and their family.

8 **Don't forget to replace negatives with positives.** Teens that come for counseling can be involved in a host of negatives such as drugs, alcohol, sexual sin, vulgar language, smoking, etc. Whatever the negative influence, replace it with a positive. If the problem is filthy music, offer some Christian music to replace it. If the problem is alcohol, talk about being filled with the Spirit. We need to provide substitutes that can help teens overcome.

9 **Don't treat all teens the same.** Certain techniques do not work with all people. What worked with Bob may not work with Sue. Be prepared to vary the technique used according to the situation and individual. The best tool for one teen may be laughter, for another it may be conviction.

10 **Don't be afraid to refer.** It is highly possible that you will come up against some circumstance that you are not qualified to handle. Maybe you're too close to the teen and their family. Or maybe the problem is too severe for your experience. Just this week I had to tell someone I counsel that he may want to see someone whose expertise is in the area of his problem.

Forty Four

10 Exercises to Help You Stay Fit

1 **Push-ups.** Get on your knees and place your palms on the floor about shoulder width apart. You can remain on your knees or stretch your legs out until you are on your toes. Keep your body straight and lower your body until the chest touches the floor, then push away from the floor until your arms are almost locked.

In the beginning you may find two or three push ups hard to do, or you may discover that your belly touches the floor before your chest. Either way, don't get discouraged! Keep working to the point of ten push-ups, then add another set and do two sets of ten.

2 **Abdominal Crunches.** Crunches are the bottom fourth of a sit-up. Lay flat on the floor and slide your feet up until they are flat on the floor. Your knees will be bent and pointing toward the ceiling. Place your hands behind your head and do a quarter sit-up concentrating on using the stomach muscles to raise your body.

Why not do regular sit-ups? Because a full sit-up puts an enormous amount of pressure on the lower back without working the abdominals any greater than with a crunch.

3 **Stair-climbing.** Use the stairs instead of the elevator whenever you can. When visiting at the hospital, take the stairs instead of the elevator. By the time you get to visit Sister Ruth on the fifth floor, you might feel like taking the

room beside hers for recuperation.

By taking the stairs you get your body to burn more calories, and use muscles it wouldn't use on the elevator. You can best decide the number of floors you can handle, but try to take the stairs for one to three floors.

4 **Squats.** Place your feet shoulder width apart and bend at your knees until the back of your legs are parallel to the ground. Try to do twenty. When you can, add another set and work up to three sets of twenty.

This exercise will help tone the entire leg area. When you get to three sets of twenty you may want to hold a book or weights in each hand for added resistance.

5 **Side-bends.** Place your hands on your hips and bend side ways to a thirty-five to forty-five degree angle. Do sets of twenty-five for each side, working up to fifty per side. This exercise works your abdominals and obliques located on the sides of your waist.

Try to get a minimum of thirty minutes of exercise three times per week. Also, don't forget to get a complete physical checkup before beginning any fitness program.

6 **Cardiovascular exercises.** Get your heart rate up by walking fast, jogging, aerobics, biking, etc. If you have never done much cardiovascular work, begin with ten minutes and work up to thirty minutes over a two month period. Try to keep your heart rate around 70% of it's maximum rate. Call a local fitness center and they will be able to help you determine the figure for your age and weight.

7 **Curls.** Grab some books or hand weights and hold them by your sides with your palms facing forward. Keep the elbows at your sides and lift your hands until they are near shoulder level. This exercise will develop the bicep area located on the front portion of your upper arm. Work up to three sets of 8-10 repetitions.

8 **Lateral raises.** Again using books or hand weights, hold them at your sides with your palms facing inward. Keeping your elbows slightly bent, lift your entire arms until they reach shoulder height. This exercise will work your entire shoulder area, especially the middle of the shoulder and the muscles surrounding the neck. Work up to three sets of 12-15.

9 **Calf raises.** Get a thick book, like a phone book for a large city and stand on it, or you may use stairs. Stand on the balls of your feet so you can stretch your heels below the edge of the book or stairs. After stretching downward, push up until you are on your toes. Do three sets of 15-20 repetitions. This exercise will work the muscles below the knee.

10 **Stretching.** When it comes to exercising, we often forget to stretch. Lack of space prevents a complete stretching program so let me encourage you to go to a local book store and get a book that includes stretching and the exercise mentioned here so you can be sure to do everything correctly. Stretching keeps you limber, feeling youthful, and increases and promotes proper blood circulation.

FORTY FIVE

10 Ways to Destroy Your Youth Group

1 Become sexually involved with teens. Nothing will destroy your ministry and the group faster or more effectively than getting sexually involved with a teen. It's disturbing to think such an encounter is even possible, but each year we hear about youth leaders who lose their ministry because of inappropriate activity.

The teens, their parents, and the church expect us to guide the group with purity. That means we should not even flirt with a teen. Don't do a single thing that hints of any sexual interest. If you sense a teen is attracted to you do whatever it takes to make it clear that nothing will ever happen between the two of you.

2 Spend very little time with teens. It's possible to get so involved in the day to day administrative aspects of ministry that we can forget it's about people, not a program. We can have a truckload of creative ideas, but if they fail to connect with the teens in a relational way they are worthless.

You can make the time quality, quantity, or both - and it doesn't have to be extraordinary. Pick up a couple of kids after school two or three times a week and play basketball, or go to the mall. Just spend time with them. It doesn't matter what you do. Teens don't care as much what you do *for* them, as they do what you do *with* them.

3 Sin with them. In order to be cool to the teens some youthworkers decide that telling dirty jokes, smoking, chewing tobacco, taking the group to a rated-R movie, or social drinking with the group will help connect them to their teens. One thing will happen for sure, the group will understand sin, and realize that it's OK to do the "small stuff." I Thessalonians 4:4 says that we should conduct ourselves in a way "holy and honorable." That means that we will not do anything with our teens that we could not talk openly with their parents about. Would they approve of the dirty joke, or R movies?

4 Cut down the church leadership in front of the group. This destroys the group by teaching them that the elders, pastors, ministers, etc., don't have to be respected. Your leaders may be the roughest, dumbest bunch of goats in the brotherhood, but it doesn't give you the right to ridicule them in front of the teens.

5 Undermine parental authority. Frankly, some parents can be jerks. Some can be hard cases. Some can seem to have no common sense when it comes their children. But regardless of how qualified we may feel they are, or are not, we have no right to tear them down to their teens.

You may find that teens seek your advice hoping that you will differ with their parents. They might work to place you between them and their parents and want you to choose. In the middle of this tension we need to remember that it is our calling to lead both parents and teens into a mature relationship with God.

6 Staying there when you're ineffective. Because of our families or creditors, we find ourselves in need of employment. But "church work" is more than simple employment, more than a job, it's a calling. Because of that we need to understand that we work for God and not man. Our occupation is different from any other on the planet because of our Employer. In light of that, we cannot allow a ministry to suffer, become stagnant, or deteriorate because we need to pay bills. If we find we are ineffective as a result of tension, stress, lack of passion, or whatever, we need to leave the ministry and find a job elsewhere.

7 Disagree with the theology of the congregation. There is no congregation that exists that will have unity on every aspect of belief. As a general rule, issues of opinion can be overlooked, but issues of theology and doctrine can cause trouble. If the church you work with differs greatly with your interpretation of God's word, go somewhere else. You will not be able to be effective for God as long as you are obligated to teach the congregation's view of Scripture when you don't really believe it.

8 Use youth ministry as a stepping stone to the pulpit. Countless youth ministers can't wait for the day that they get to preach. They view youth ministry as a temporary desert before entering the promised land of the pulpit. While there's nothing wrong with aspiring to preach if that is where God is leading, we must have a passion for the youth we work with. It's hard to serve effectively where you are when you're longing to be in another position.

9 Teach teens to follow you and not Jesus. I don't know of any youth worker who intentionally tries to get teens to follow after him or her. But unintentionally we may find that a teen's commitment is in direct proportion to the amount of attention we pay him. That's why so many graduate the youth group and graduate from God as well.

Our goal is for teens to follow Jesus with or without our presence. By introducing them to Jesus we can be assured that their faith is in Him and not in us.

10 Put your group in a bubble. In an effort to protect our teens from the world, we may shelter them from some things that would help them grow. As a church we may find ourselves not participating with other churches because we don't want the group to face different doctrinal issues.

We may decide to shelter the group by just doing safe things that won't result in stretching or testing our comfort zones. The truth is that no aspect of a teens world is safe and if we show that the way the church deals with problems is to ignore them, we may find our teens ill-equipped to face the daily dangers.

FORTY SIX

10 Tips Teens Need to Know How to do Before Leaving the Group

1 How to love the Lord with all their heart, soul, mind and strength. Those four characteristics balance lives and allow teens to experience balanced spirituality. The heart speaks of our emotions. Soul speaks of our spirit. Mind speaks of our intellect. And strength speaks of our bodies. Before teens graduate from your group make sure they have each area of focus.

2 How to love their neighbor as themselves. Most insults, gossip, back biting, etc. stem from insecurity or inferiority. Teach teens just how precious they are to God and to use that fact as a motivation to treat others as precious. Remind them of the teaching of the good Samaritan in Luke 17. The question is not "Who is my neighbor," but "Am I being a neighbor?"

3 How to pray and have faith that God will answer those prayers. How many times have we prayed and then said, "I don't think God will do that?" James 1:6-7 makes it clear that a doubter shouldn't expect anything. In contrast, the prayer of faith is able to bring incredible things from the hand of God.

When we don't trust God it means we trust ourselves. Have your group not only keep a prayer journal, but make sure they mark the answered prayers. You might decide to have a weekly testimony period for those who may want to share how God has answered their prayers that week.

4 **How to worship and experience it.** Teens may think worship equates to a pew-filled auditorium on Sunday mornings. Jesus made it clear in John 4 that worship is not about a time or place but about a relationship with the Almighty.

Worship places value on God. Specifically, worship is a heart expression through word, song or thought that attributes glory to God. Pews aren't needed to sit in His presence. A worship leader isn't required for teens to present their worship to the Lord. Teach your teens the power of a humble spirit, bent knees, and open expression to the Father.

5 **How to have a personal relationship with God.** Jesus said, "Follow me." That statement automatically excludes everyone and everything else. It is amazing and scary just how dependant a group's faith can be in a person instead of God. Do the teens hang on our every word or His every word? Do they make spiritual decisions on their own, or only with our prompting? Do teens know what's right because *they* believe it, or do they just repeat the facts they have been taught?

6 **How to keep their faith in God for an eternity.** After the seniors graduate, they will enter a new world of freedom. And with that freedom comes temptation. With no parents looking over their shoulders every minute "no one will ever know." New surroundings will create a desire to fit in and be accepted. Teens may find themselves in classes where the professor thinks God is a joke, or at best a myth. What will happen to the teen's faith then? How strong will they be? How firmly will they stand?

Prepare your group by helping them develop not only a first hand faith, but a firm faith. Make them aware of the challenges before them. Provide practical teaching and experiences that will stay with them long after they leave your care.

7 **How to have respect for authority.** Teens can't wait for the freedom we just talked about. But there is no absolute freedom. Life comes with rules. Professors expect on-time students, completed term papers, and completed final exams. The law expects the speed limit to be followed, no stealing, and no murdering.

Bucking the system and being a rebel won't work in the world, and it's not what God wants. Get your group ready for the "real world" by training them in "Yes, Sir," and "Yes,

Maam."

8 **How to study the Bible.** This seems like a no-brainer, but most teens have no clue about how to get the most from Bible study. Show them how to use the concordance in the back of their Bibles. Explain commentaries, the languages the Book was originally written in, and the importance of looking at a passage in its context. All of that stuff might sound heavy to a teen, but it will mean the difference between reading the Bible with confusion, or reading it with understanding.

9 **How to share the good news of Jesus.** Teens list various reasons for not talking about Jesus: "I'm too scared." I don't know enough." "My life isn't consistent enough." Make faith sharing as easy as possible. There has never been a seminar on "How to invite your friends to a football game." Why? Because it's natural. Teach teens that the gospel should be as natural as any other invitation.

10 **How to win over temptation.** No one is free from temptation, so how can we win? The book of James provides some needed support. First, James tells us how sin operates, so we can be aware of its process (1:12-15). Later, he makes it clear that we need to resist the Devil and he will run from us (4:7). Then we run from Satan into the hands of God, who happens to be running toward us as well (4:8)!

Arm your teens with this battle plan because it is guaranteed to work - if they'll use it.

As students leave your group for a new chapter in life, give them something they can take with them. It may be a book, a list of absolute truths, or a personal note challenging each student to be strong. Whatever you choose to do, make it special. Make it something that lets him or her know that you are glad they were part of your group.

FORTY SEVEN

10 TIPS TO A JOY-FILLED YOUTH MINISTRY

1 **Stay close to God.** As rigid as some people feel God is, isn't it amazing at how things go smoothly when we are close to Him. When we follow His ways we receive blessings as a result. When we venture out on our own, we receive negative consequences.

Common sense question: Do we get more joy from blessings or consequences? So how do we stay close to God so we can gain the blessing of His presence? Go to the next tip.

2 **Have a daily quiet time.** Owen Carr put it perfectly, "A day without prayer is a boast against God." There is no need to make this a complex ritual. Get a daily devotional book, or workbook, or follow a simple pattern. One I like includes reading a passage and meditating on it for a few minutes to consider what God is trying to say to me through His Word. Then I think of a song that relates to the verse(s) and quote the lyrics or sing them as praise to the Father. Finally, I say a prayer that reflects the verse and how I want to surrender to God on the area studied. (You'll get 10 of these on page 153).

3 **Show interest in others.** We all know that when we place our focus on others, we think less about ourselves. Our problems suddenly become insignificant. A peace and con-

tentment comes from letting go of ourselves and using our energy to benefit another. Philippians 4:3 tells us to look at the interests of others and not only at our own interests.

4 **Stick to a savings plan and stay out of debt.** Alright, alright! Ministry is not the best place to do those two things, but financial woes always get us down. The best way to stay debt free is to be debt free in the first place. But for the sake of argument let's imagine that you have some debt and no savings plan. Allow me to suggest three things.

1. Do not put anything else on credit. If you don't have the cash for it, then don't get it.
2. Pay off the existing debt from the smallest to the largest. Put as much toward your debt each month as you can.
3. Start a consistent savings plan even if it's $10 a month. Stick with it and when your debts are paid increase your saving (page 132).

5 **Be creative.** There's nothing fun about being tied down physically, emotionally, or intellectually. In ministry we need to set ourselves free to be creative. Approach lessons from a different angle. Have teens sit in your chair when they come in your office. Watch the scene from Dead Poets Society when Robin Williams has all his students stand on the desk as see things from a new perspective. Doesn't the thought of that kind of living bring joy to you?

6 **Give thanks and be grateful for what you have.** When we live in the land of "I want" we find that we are rarely satisfied. No matter how much we accumulate or the accolades we gather there always seems to be something else we want. Combat the "I want" feelings with thanksgiving. Make a simple list of the things you have that most people on the planet don't have, yet most of us take for granted. Things like a place to live, freedom, food and clothing. Keep the list on you at all times and when the "I want" thoughts enter take out the list and reflect on what you already have.

7 **Listen to the wisdom of others and act on it.** In our do-it-yourself society we may start to think that if we can't do it alone, it's not worth doing. On the contrary. Keep an ear open for those who have lived and made the mistakes you want to avoid, and for those who reap the blessings you desire. Proverbs 13:20 says that he who walks with the wise will grow wise.

8 **Cultivate a great attitude.** A few people on this planet seem to be born with a great personality and attitude. The rest of us have to work on it. Negativity sucks the joy out of life. Being positive helps us see the rainbow in the middle of the storm.

Let's work on our attitudes by recognizing what sets us off, or makes us lose focus. When those moments come we need to immediately replace the negative with the positive. The Holy Spirit said it best when through Paul he wrote, "Think about everything good all the time" (Philippians 4:8, paraphrased).

9 **Spend time away from ministry.** Since Jesus said He would give us rest, why won't all of His followers give us a moment of peace? I used to feel guilty about days off (key words: used to). But now I realize that I need time away from my job - not God - if I am going to stay productive. You do as well. Schedule one day a week to "forget" about ministry. Don't plan, or study, or discover the greatest youth program in history. Relax and let nothing except an emergency pull you from that time. Sure some folks might get upset about the way "you never work." When he does invite him to host the next teen lock-in.

10 **Be a giver.** Jesus told us that the one who gives get a bigger blessing than the one who receives. Why do you think that's true? Write your three answers below and discover your final tip for joy:

1.

2.

3.

Forty Eight

10 Techniques for Recognizing Burnout

1 **"I feel like there is far too much responsibility on my shoulders."** It's tough having your name on every project. You know that if something goes wrong you get the blame. It's also hard feeling like things might not go well if you are not involved.

Reserve the right to say "No" when your plate is full. And don't go on a guilt trip if you can't accept every responsibility in the church.

2 **"I am constantly frustrated with my ministry."** Leaders won't approve an increased budget? Parents blaming you for their teen's drug problem? The church thinks youth ministry is a teenage babysitting service? What is your personal frustration? When you stay disappointed or irritated with the ministry, burnout awaits us. We need to relax and work on the areas that have a solution and let go of the ones that don't.

3 **"I feel alienated from the rest of the staff."** Cliques don't just happen in high school. They can occur in ministry as well. The "more visual" ministries may seem to be popular, and you may feel left out. Or the other ministries may appear to receive a lot of attention from the pulpit and publications, while you and the youth get placed on an obscure bulletin

board.

Be proactive about forming relationships with the staff. If you sense a distance, then close the gap. Invite other staff members out to lunch, or over to your house for a meal. Do whatever it take to insure all of you are on the same team.

4 **"There is not enough time in the day to do my ministry properly."** If time seems a foe rather than a friend, you will find yourself working more and more hours while neglecting other important areas of life.

We need to prioritize our days and work on the crucial jobs, while handing off the non-crucial. If we don't have enough time, it's usually because we weigh each ministry aspect equally.

5 **"I neglect my family for my ministry."** Do we want our children to grow up thinking we loved other kids, more than our own? Ignoring the family leads to burnout at God's house and our house.

Let's encourage our families to be honest about the time we are spending with them. We may discover that even when we are at home, we are thinking about our jobs and they will pick up on that. Set a minimum number of hours per week spent with the family at non-ministry related times and stick with it.

6 **"I am not sleeping well and have a lack of energy."** A few months ago I went to see my doctor (the first time in fourteen years). I felt weak and tired all the time. After all the blood work and other tests, the doctor pronounced me incredibly healthy. Then we started reviewing my schedule and he attributed my fatigue to stress. Have you ever felt that way? If so it may not be a diet or exercise problem, but a stress related problem. Call your physician and ask him or her to suggest ways to lower your stress levels.

7 **"I find myself leaving God out of my day."** Ministry is being about our Father's business. If we leave Him out, we don't have a ministry, just a program powered by human strength. When we leave God out we get burned out because we are trying to rely on us instead of Him. Even if it just feels like you're going through the motions, spend at least 15 minutes a day in the Lord's presence without it relating to anything but your personal relationship with Him. Talk freely and openly to Him about the distance you sense and the need

to have Him empower your ministry.

8 **"I never have a moment to myself."** There is no clocking out in ministry. Everyone has a right to call you at any time of the night or day regardless of convenience. If you are a volunteer youth worker it can seem even worse. You work a full time job, then come home to another job.

Full timers: When you know you have busy nights, take some time off during the day. Part timers or volunteers: Let your people know the teens can call anytime, but ministry questions or dilemmas can only be handled three nights a week.

9 **"Over half the stuff I have to do has nothing to do with my ministry."** Sure, we were hired for youth ministry, but that doesn't mean the church leaders don't expect you to have the budget report collated by Sunday at 4 p.m.

Avoid anything that does not directly tie into your ministry. As a general rule, if people think you might be willing to take a job, they will give it to you. Is it so bad to be known for knocking yourself out in your ministry but being noncommittal in other areas?

10 **"I'm sick of these kids."** Generally those words are uttered by every youth minister in the nation after "summer vacation." But if we find ourselves saying that all year round - watch out!

Develop friendships outside the group. Have adult friends that you hang out with who don't have teens, and do have common interests with you. Forcing yourself to be with the teens all the time is not the way to prevent burnout, but will insure it.

> Burn out can make you burn up with pride, bitterness, anger and a number of other ungodly reactions. Set aside time each week to evaluate yourself spiritually and physically to protect yourself from life's heat.

FORTY NINE

10 Quiet Time Tools

When time is pressing don't cancel your time with God. Use one of these quiet time suggestions to meditate on the Lord. They're simple, yet powerful: Read the Passage, sing a song of praise in response, and pray for the Father to instill the principle in your life.

1 **Principle:**Our God is Worthy of All Praise
Passage: Psalm 66:1-5
Praise: "Awesome God" by Rich Mullins
Prayer: *Father, I give you praise for who you are. You are worthy of all praise and honor. Forgive me for the times when I steal your glory. May my life, its words and its action, reflect You and point back to You.*

2 **Principle:** God is the Creator of All Things
Passage: Genesis 1
Praise: "We Bow Down" by Twila Paris
Prayer: *Father, Open my eyes to see each person, animal, or plant as a reflection of Your power to create and sustain life. Let me see myself as a wonder of your creation, formed and shaped in Your image for Your purposes.*

3 **Principle:** The Lord Can Bring Peace Out of Chaos
Passage: Matthew 8:23-27
Praise: "Peace, Perfect Peace" by Bickersteth & Caldbeck
Prayer: *Father, calm my life. In moments when life feels like a stormy sea, send Your peace. Fill my heart with the comfort and peace that only You can provide.*

4 **Principle:** Christ Paid the Price

Passage: Romans 5:1-11

Praise: "Amazing Grace" by John Newton

Prayer: *Father, thank you for Your grace. My sin is great, but Your grace is greater. I can't imagine why You allowed Jesus to die for me. I am unworthy and undeserving, but that's why it's called grace. Thank you for Your gift of love so that even my worst sin would go unpunished.*

5 **Principle:** The Blessing of Friends

Passage: Proverbs 17:17

Praise: "Friends" by Michael W. Smith

Prayer: *Father, I want to thank You for friends. When I am down, You use them to lift me up. When I am weak, You use them to make me strong. When I am sad, You provide their shoulder to cry on. When I am tempted, You allow their accountability to keep me focused.*

6 **Principle:** The Surrendered Life

Passage: Mark 10:28-31

Praise: "All to Jesus I Surrender" by Venter & Weeden

Prayer: *Father, why can't I seem to lay everything in Your hands. In this moment Lord, I wave the white flag of surrender. I lay down my desires and pick up Your desires. I lay down my wants, and pick up Your wishes. Father, remind me of the sacrifice that Jesus made which causes me to respond with a surrendered life.*

7 **Principle:** The Good News of Jesus

Passage: 1 Corinthians 15:1-4

Praise: "Lord, I Lift Your Name On High" by Rick Founds

Prayer: *Father, make my life good news to others. Let me live in the simple pure message of the gospel. Jesus lived, died, and rose so I could be forgiven. Thank you for saving my life. Let the impact of that thought move me toward others so they can receive the same blessing of salvation.*

8 **Principle:** Become a Servant
Passage: Philippians 2:6-11
Praise: "Make Me a Servant" - traditional
Prayer: *Father, let me see the difference between service and serve us. I admit that I enjoy being served more than serving. Let me take the less prestigeous seat at the table. Let my heart be filled with joy when some one else gets the credit. Let me follow the example of my Lord Jesus when He rose from the table, wrapped a towel around Himself, and washed feet.*

9 **Principle:** Praise Him Freely
Passage: Psalm 100
Praise: "Doxology" by Ken & Psalter
Prayer: *Father, I don't praise You enough. How easy it is to look around and complain. Father, take away my critical spirit and replace it with praise for You. Help me see You when others miss You. From the birds on the wind to the flowers of spring let my mouth pour out praise to You.*

10 **Principle:** The Blood of Jesus Purifies
Passage: Hebrews 9:1-14
Praise: "Nothing But the Blood of Jesus" by Robert Lowery
Prayer: *Father, I thank You for my not having to offer sacrifices on an altar. May my life be on the altar since Christ became a sacrifice for me. Correct me when I start feeling like I earned part of my salvation, and remind me that only the blood of Jesus can wash away sin. Thank You for that blood.*

FIFTY

10 Tools to Go Deep with God

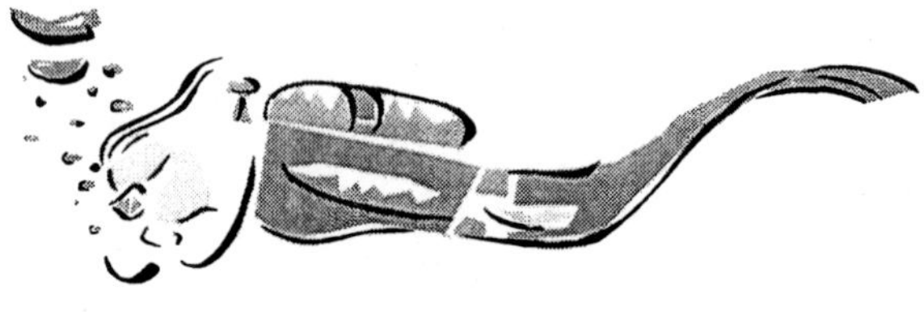

1 **Walk with Him.** "Enoch walked with God... (Genesis 5:24a). This picture of peace expresses the type of relationship we long to have with God. Walking depicts an intimate friendship among two like individuals. The more we become like Him the more we walk with Him.

Walking also brings to mind a picture of His presence. Live each moment with the knowledge of His nearness. Going deep with God means more than a casual 10 minute stroll, it calls for constant connection.

2 **Talk with Him.** "The Lord would speak with Moses face to face, as a man speaks with his friend..." Exodus 33:11. Jim Cymbala writes in *Fresh Wind, Fresh Fire,* "Does anyone really think that America today is lacking preachers, books, Bible translations, and neat doctrinal statements? What we really lack is the passion to call upon the name of the Lord until He opens the heavens and shows Himself powerful."

When we get bold enough to get face to face and really talk with Him instead of sharing shallow requests, we will find His power flowing through our ministries like open flood gates.

3 **Become a worshiper.** "Yet a time is coming and has now come when the true worshipers will worship the Father in spirit and truth, for they are the kind of worshipers the Father seeks" John 4:23. God looks for worshipers. He seeks

them. Sometimes we get caught up in the idea of performing acts of worship, and we forget to worship. God isn't looking for worship, but worshipers. He doesn't want a performance, but the participating hearts of His people. Become a worshiper by refusing to hold anything back when it comes to expressing your praise to Him.

4 **Get faith based, not sight-based.** "And he was amazed at their lack of faith" Mark 6:6. "When Jesus heard this, he was amazed at him, and turning to the crowd following him, he said, 'I tell you, I have not found such great faith even in Israel'." Luke 7:9. Two times in scripture we find Jesus amazed and they both had to do with faith. Once small faith amazed Him - negative. One time great faith amazed Him - positive.

Let's develop a trust in God that will cause Him to gather heaven's inhabitants, point at our lives and say, "Wow, they've got amazing faith!"

5 **Give sacrificially.** "But just as you excel in everything—in faith, in speech, in knowledge, in complete earnestness and in your love for us - see that you also excel in this grace of giving" (2 Corinthians 8:7). Go deep into your wallet and give by faith. Bible study and prayer come as natural extensions of our walk with God, but giving is tough. Most of us spend money without thought, and give it the same way. David said that he would do nothing for God that cost him nothing. Do we find our giving is a cost to our lives, or do we view it as just another bill in the pile?

6 **Be holy and honorable.** "It is God's will that you should be sanctified: that you should avoid sexual immorality; that each of you should learn to control his own body in a way that is holy and honorable" (I Thessalonians 4:3-4). Claiming to be a Christian, and living as one, are two different things. We can take our relationship with God to a different level by living in such a way that we would be willing to share any aspect of our life openly and without shame. We should be able to tell every detailed action or thought from our lives from morning till night without fear.

7 **Rejoice in all circumstances.** "Rejoice in the Lord always; I will say it again, rejoice" (Philippians 4:4). Each moment of each day contains a praise moment. By training ourselves to rejoice all the time, God will enable us to see the blessings in

the middle of the curse. No matter how small something good may seem, let's immediately lift up praise to the God of all good things who delivered the moment.

8 **Take the Word to heart.** "For the word of God is living and active. Sharper than any double-edged sword, it penetrates even to dividing soul and spirit, joints and marrow; it judges the thoughts and attitudes of the heart" (Hebrews 11:4). Let God's Word do its work. It convicts and instructs us at the same time. Yet, if we are not careful, we will read it and miss the meaning. We may find ourselves learning facts and failing to discover application. It's tempting to study for a lesson or devotional, but not for personal maturity.

9 **Welcome God's transforming power.** "And we, who with unveiled faces all reflect the Lord's glory, are being transformed into his likeness with ever-increasing glory, which comes from the Lord, who is the Spirit" (2 Corinthians 3:18). We can't be satisfied with remaining where we are in Him. Let's crave transformation, constantly asking the Father to make us more like the Son.

10 **Live in the sufficiency of His grace.** "My grace is sufficient for you, for my power is made perfect in weakness" (2 Corinthians 12:9). When Paul had a "thorn in the flesh" he pleaded with God to take it way. God's response? "My grace is sufficient for you." Regardless of how unfair life may seem, we are saved. No matter how many parents rise up against you, or how many heathen teens occupy the group in a given summer, you belong to Him. That one guarantee, God says, should be enough to sustain you throughout any problem or trial - and you have to be deep with God to live on that level.

For information about other Teen Life Products call or write us at:

Teen Life Ministries
3009 Willow Lane Dr
Montgomery, AL 36109
(334)277-7726

Or visit us online:

www.TeenLifeMinistries.com
TLM@teenlifeministries.com